INTEGRATING
PRIMITIVE REFLEXES
THROUGH PLAY AND EXERCISE

AN INTERACTIVE GUIDE TO THE
ASYMMETRICAL TONIC NECK REFLEX (ATNR)

KOKEB GIRMA MCDONALD, OTR/L
OCCUPATIONAL THERAPIST REGISTERED AND LICENSED

DEDICATION

MY HUSBAND

Thank you for your love and support. Thank you for being on this life journey with me. Your dedication to making a positive difference in the world continues to inspire me daily. I love you!

PARENTS AND CAREGIVERS

The *Integrating Primitive Reflexes Integration Through Play and Exercise* series is dedicated to all parents and caregivers of children with special needs. You take on more than most parents and continuously strive to better the future of your children, often without the support you and your children need. I hope the information I share eases your challenging journey and offers you a useful tool for incorporating helpful exercises into your home routine. Remember, you are not alone!

TEACHERS

This series is also for all teachers. You are some of our children's primary influencers and game changers. Outside of the home, you have the most impact on our children's development. Helping you to create a safe and effective classroom for all children is my main goal.

FELLOW SERVICE PROVIDERS

For my fellow occupational therapists and service providers, you work hard to meet the needs of your clients, often not seeing the fruits of your labor. Working alongside you has been a great privilege and is what pushes me to continue finding effective solutions for our clients and their families every day. Together, we can make a difference!

FREE GIFT

Thank you for purchasing our book

As a special thank you, we'd love to gift you with FREE companion resources to help you on your journey!

DOWNLOAD NOW

RITP.INFO/ATNR-BOOK

Transform your Treatment Plans ANYWHERE, ANYTIME!

Access to 100+ exercises to address retained reflexes

Collect exercises together into easy to access playlists

Share playlists with other app users!

Kid friendly easy-to-follow videos and instructions right in your pocket!

Access to exclusive learning videos by Kokeb Mcdonald, OTR/L & Author

DOWNLOAD OUR APP NOW

RITP.INFO/APP

LEARN MORE

RITP.INFO/CERTIFICATION

Are you a Service Provider ready to grow?

Explore our Reflex Integration Through Play™ Certification Program!

 ## Say Hello to...

- Refining and expanding your clinical skills to effectively address the most complex developmental delays
- Broadening your professional and business opportunities available to you as a therapist
- Having a done-for-you treatment and at-home plan highly targeted to treat children with developmental delays

The Program Includes

In-Depth Courses & Training

Live Support Calls

Collaborative Community

Access to Mobile App

Done-For-You Treatment Plans

Step-by-Step

Play-Based Exercises

American Occupational Therapy Association

Approved Provider

LEARN MORE

RITP.INFO/FAMILY

Skyrocket your Child's Progress at HOME!

As a parent, do you...

- See developmental challenges in your child and don't know where to start?
- Want to accelerate your child's therapy program?
- Feel overwhelmed with at-home movement plans and want to make it more fun?

We want to support you with our Reflex Integration Through Play™ Family Bundle!

Our Family Bundle Includes:

Hours of training on play-based reflex integration tailored to a home environment

In-depth on-demand course covering retained reflexes & their impact on your child

Access to our Mobile App (100+ exercise instructions!)

Access to a private membership community

Bring Reflex Integration Through Play™ to Your School!

Are you an educator looking to provide fun movement breaks & sensory diet programs for your students?

Your Students Will...

- Grow in their energy levels
- Improve their attention span and academic performance
- Progress in their social skills and physical abilities

LEARN MORE

RITP.INFO/SCHOOL

TABLE OF CONTENTS

BALL GAMES:
BOUNDING, CATCHING, HITTING, AND THROWING

GAMES AND SPORTS

PREFACE

Welcome to *An Interactive Guide to Asymmetrical Tonic Neck Reflex (ATNR)*, the second book in the series *Integrating Primitive Reflexes Through Play and Exercise*. I hope you'll find these exercises fun and useful.

If this is your first experience with this series, please also check out the **first book on the Moro Reflex**. Much of the information in this book, such as the introduction, reflex descriptions, and definitions, is similar to that in the previous book. Working first on the Moro Reflex may also be essential to success with the exercises for the ATNR included in this book. If you have read the first book and understand primitive reflexes and their benefits and simply want to focus on the ATNR, you can skip to Chapter 2, and begin the home program.

Many parents spend time reading about research and findings but are left more confused and overwhelmed than they were before, as much of the information available is geared toward professionals. What most parents need is a practical guide that relies on research yet is written in terms they can understand and easily put to use. After publishing the first book in this series on the Moro Reflex, I received positive feedback from several parents, teachers, and service providers who said that the simple, step-by-step instructions were helping them. They also reported that they had been looking for a simple guide with clear instructions but, until now, had not been able to find one. If you are one of these parents, you know what it feels like to balance your work, life, parental duties, and still make sure you are providing the best possible support for your child's developmental needs. This book is mainly for you.

The books in this series are not presented in any specific order. If you choose, you can work on many reflexes at the same time or in any sequence. However, if you suspect your child may have Moro Reflex retention, for example, I highly recommend you start with that reflex. Since the Moro Reflex affects all of our senses, including our fight and flight response, it is best to start calming the nervous system before tackling the challenge of integrating other reflexes, which can be stressful; however, you do not need to have the Moro Reflex fully integrated to begin working on other reflexes.

While you may begin working on any reflex—or multiple reflexes—as you first utilize this series, it is essential that you know the retention of one reflex often leads to the retention of another reflex. It is not always clear which reflex is dominating the body at a given time. To be safe, I recommend screening for and working on *all* primitive reflexes with a trained specialist. With the results of comprehensive screening, you will be better informed and able to implement these guidebooks for optimal results. In the meantime, you can safely incorporate these fun games and activities into your home or classroom routine in a way that makes sense for you and your child, and observe your child's performance. I chose these specific exercises because they are easy to implement and allow for easy observation of the retained reflex pattern when it is present in the body. Plus, they are fun, and parents can participate in at-home exercises, allowing for healthy play. A win-win for all!

I hope you'll find the information and exercises in this book helpful on your journey to support the development of the children with whom you work. I also invite you to join our growing community of parents, teachers, and therapists in our private Facebook group at https://www.facebook.com/integratingreflexes. There you'll find discussions and further information about our reflex book series. You can also visit our main site to subscribe to our newsletters and get informed when the next book is available.

Kokeb Girma McDonald, OTR/L
California, 2020

INTRODUCTION

As a working parent, I can testify that it is hard to come home from a busy workday and do therapeutic exercises with a child. You are tired, and your child is fatigued from a hectic day at school. The last thing any parent wants to do is start an activity a child will fight over. Even as a trained pediatric occupational therapist, I am challenged when I make these home exercises a chore for my child, and there is less motivation to do them when their benefits are not fully understood. The best home-based programs are those that are fun, playful, and exploratory as well as therapeutic. It takes creativity and professional guidance to set up a successful home program that can be easily carried out.

Children learn through play and repetition, and the best interventions are those that incorporate these activities in the children's natural setting: their home. For a therapeutic team to create effective home programs, treatment plans should be the result of a collaboration between parents and therapists. Therapists guide a child's development more effectively if they partner with parents in the treatment planning and execution processes. In most cases, a child receives a weekly or bi-weekly, one-on-one therapy session with little to no interaction between the parents and therapist. While this approach can be helpful to some degree, it will not be as effective as a team approach. Like rowing a boat, you will get to your destination faster and with less energy when everyone on the crew works together.

Since parents are their children's first teachers and are the most likely to motivate and influence them, they are well suited to incorporate movement recommendations throughout the week. In this way, parents can (1) provide needed repetition of exercises and (2) easily discern which interventions are working well, while providing feedback to the therapist regularly. This integrated approach not only helps to achieve results more quickly, but it also reduces the number of therapy sessions needed—and therefore reduces the total cost incurred by parents. Furthermore, when parent-therapist collaboration is weak, the therapist can only rely on data collected during an individual therapy session in a controlled environment as opposed to assessing skills that are practiced in the child's home life. This gap in data may lead to termination of a potentially effective intervention that would have been beneficial were it carried out.

In this second book of the series, I have compiled simple, step-by-step therapeutic exercises that focus on the Asymmetrical Tonic Neck Reflex (ATNR), one of the primary reflexes. These exercises can be used by parents, teachers, and service providers, whether at home, at school, or in the office. If you are a parent, make sure to consult your child's occupational therapist or physician before you begin any intervention program or modify any program given to you by your clinician.

The goal of this handbook is threefold:

1. **Be a resource for service providers.** This book is designed to provide an accessible resource for the specialist working to integrate the Asymmetrical Tonic Neck Reflex (ATNR). It includes a brief explanation of the ATNR, its onset and integration, its benefits, and the symptoms that arise when this primary reflex does not become integrated.

2. **Offer simple, step-by-step therapeutic home exercises.** This handbook includes a menu of simple therapeutic exercises, clear goals, and a progress-tracking guide for a home-based program created to meet the needs of both parents and their children.

3. **Provide an easy-to-use training manual for parents and teachers.** The best intervention is one that carries over from the therapeutic setting into the home and classroom. By implementing exercises that can be learned easily and quickly, parents and teachers provide the needed repetition and consistency in a therapeutic routine, and, in turn, encourage faster results. Tracking charts provided in the appendix allow

parents and service providers to easily work on and track the same goals.

*This program is not intended as medical advice and should be implemented with the help of a trained service provider.

**This handbook should not be used to diagnose any condition or disease or replace other therapeutic reflex integration programs.

WHAT ARE PRIMITIVE REFLEXES?

Reflexes are normal, involuntary movement patterns that promote motor learning and sensory integration. Motor learning is a neurological ability to learn new movement skills through practice and repetition. Sensory integration is the mind's and body's ability to perceive internal and external information through the senses and to learn, respond, and adapt accordingly. Our senses include but are not limited to sight, hearing, taste, smell, touch, vestibular (sense of movement and balance), and proprioceptive (body awareness).

Primitive reflexes are involuntary movement patterns that are present at birth and become integrated or "dormant" before a child reaches 12 months of age. Most reflexes become integrated into a pattern of movement after infancy, so more mature and voluntary movements can emerge. However, sometimes reflexes do not become integrated and interfere with a child's ability to develop an appropriate foundation for stability and mobility. Therefore, a child without integrated primitive reflexes may learn faulty and maladaptive movement patterns (Oden, 2004). Trained therapists can observe these faulty responses by the way a child reacts, behaves, and moves. An effective way to address this interference in reflex integration is to help the child recreate activities a typically developing child would have performed in order to integrate reflexes. Repetition of such therapeutic exercises will give the child a second chance to reintegrate the reflexes and rewire the brain-body connection.

CHAPTER 1

PRIMITIVE REFLEXES AND THEIR BENEFITS

Primitive reflexes are involuntary movement patterns controlled by the brain stem and executed without reaching the cortical or "conscious" part of the brain. Primitive reflexes emerge in utero and mostly integrate before a child reaches approximately 12 months of age. These reflexes include the Moro Reflex, Rooting Reflex, Palmar (Grasp) Reflex, Asymmetrical Tonic Neck Reflex (ATNR), Spinal Galant Reflex, Tonic Labyrinthine Reflex (TLR), Symmetrical Tonic Neck Reflex (STNR), and more.

Primitive reflexes are necessary during the birthing process, and are key to the infant's first-year survival. Instinctively, infants respond to the world via the primitive reflexes. Together, the primitive reflexes help infants move through the birth canal, take their first breath, instinctively withdraw from hazardous stimuli, urinate, creep, grasp, lift their heads, open their mouth, suck and swallow, and kick. Each primitive reflex has its own benefits and is a building block to an infant's future movement patterns and how he or she perceives the world via the senses. Therefore, primitive reflexes also impact emotional development. In a healthy and typically developing brain, the infant slowly begins to integrate these reflexes naturally, and they become dormant, so a more mature reflex pattern called the "postural reflexes" can develop.

Postural reflexes are mature patterns of responses that control balance, motor coordination, and sensory motor development. Postural reflexes succeed primitive reflexes, and retention of the latter will affect the child's development. Therefore, it is challenging to work on a child's postural reflexes, without first going back and making sure the brain has integrated the primitive reflexes. For this reason, therapists should start treatment with primitive reflex screening and integration programs to set a solid developmental foundation.

In cases where there is the presence of trauma, genetic abnormality, chronic illness, developmental delays, or pregnancy or birthing complications, primitive reflexes may still be actively present in the child's body. If primitive reflexes are actively present when they should be inhibited, they are called "retained reflexes." **Retained reflexes** will continue to cause involuntary movement patterns or physical responses that will in turn cause faulty learning processes. Also, as the baby continues to grow, he or she may begin to perceive the world in an immature way, and behavioral challenges may follow when primitive reflexes are actively present.

When a child's brain is healthy and developing typically, maturation and growth are automatic. The child goes through natural and instinctive movement patterns that assist the brain in learning and integrating primitive reflexes. We see confusion in the brain when the child either does not go through the typical milestones or skips them altogether. For example, when a child moves from sitting to walking but skips the crawling phase, an essential process for brain integration, this jump in development can confuse further development that requires the right and left brain to coordinate to execute more advanced movements.

Every natural developmental stage is necessary, and the brain uses each one for critical learning and essential growth. Similarly, a skilled therapist can integrate retained reflexes by following the natural developmental process, and mimicking activities and movements that were missed or done incorrectly in the child's previous stages to help the brain rewire itself. This book will focus on the Asymmetrical Tonic Neck Reflex (ATNR), its benefits, and the signs and symptoms we observe when it is retained in the body.

CHAPTER 2

WHAT IS THE ASYMMETRICAL TONIC NECK REFLEX (ATNR)

A. ONSET AND PATTERNS OF THE ASYMMETRICAL TONIC NECK REFLEX

The Asymmetrical Tonic Neck Reflex (ATNR) is a primitive reflex pattern, typically emerging in utero (at approximately 18 weeks) that is fully present at birth and integrates at approximately six months after birth. It is an involuntary reaction in response to the head turning to the right or left.

At the beginning of the infant's life, the head may turn from side to side reflexively, but, as the infant develops and grows, he/she will begin to respond to sensory stimuli, such as touch, sound, or sight. These sensory stimuli can initiate the head turning to the side, triggering the ATNR pattern.

Sensory stimuli that may cause the head to turn include:

- sound (auditory),

- light (vision),

- touch (tactile).

The Asymmetrical Tonic Neck Reflex becomes triggered when the head turns to the right or to the left.

Image #1: The Asymmetrical Tonic Neck Reflex Pattern

Motor responses include:

- extension of the arm and leg that the head turns toward

- and flexing of the opposite arm and leg from which the head turns away.

Additional physical responses include the following:

- the ear (auditory) and the eye (sight), the head turns toward, become acutely focused.

- the ear (auditory) and the eye (sight), the head turns away from, become slightly dormant.

- the vestibular system, located in the inner ear, which affects balance and orientation, will be influenced by the movement of the head.

Image #2: The ear and the eye the head
turns toward become acutely focused.

B. BENEFITS OF THE ASYMMETRICAL TONIC NECK REFLEX (ATNR)

The Asymmetrical Tonic Neck Reflex (ATNR), also known as *the learning reflex*, is an essential reflex pattern which directly and indirectly affects early life experiences and developmental skills.

BIRTHING PROCESS

The ATNR is a primitive reflex pattern that emerges in utero and is present during birth. For example, the kicking movement pattern, which resembles the ATNR, is frequently observed in utero through ultrasound. During the birthing stage, the ATNR prepares the infant for transitional movement through the birth canal and, in conjunction with other primitive reflexes, assists in passing through the birth canal.

CROSSING MIDLINE

Crossing midline is the body's ability to cross the middle of the body to reach the opposite side, which includes using the arms, legs, vision (sight), hearing (auditory), and vestibular system. Crossing the midline is essential to the development of movement coordination, spatial awareness, cognitive development, and brain development of a child. When performing a movement task that requires both parts of the body to move together, the right and left sides of the body need to cross the midline to coordinate a movement pattern, such as crawling, walking, brushing teeth, dressing, combing hair, reading, writing, sports, and more. The right and left sides of the brain have to communicate well to organize and coordinate a specific movement. When primitive reflexes are retained, there will be a lag in movement, delayed responses, confusion, or inability to perform the task entirely.

The Asymmetrical Tonic Neck Reflex (ATNR) also influences the coordination of the left and right hemispheres of the brain, and the development of one-side dominance (think right- or left-handedness). One-side dominance is critical for motor learning and the ability to take actions without concentrating on them (called "automaticity"). Without automaticity, movements must be consciously executed making them cumbersome and tiring. For example, if there is lack of one-side dominance, a child may continuously switch hands when writing, relying on conscious memory for letter formation. In this way, the child will spend additional time relearning letter formation rather than understanding what he or she is writing. Failure to develop one-side dominance can also lead to fatigue, lack of focus, lack of language fluency, and frustration.

VISUAL SKILLS

Any reflex pattern that moves the head, including the ATNR, affects and influences visual skills development. In this book, we will focus on visual skills the ATNR partially influences. If vision skills are an area of concern, consider working on more reflexes, such as the Moro Reflex, Symmetrical Tonic Neck Reflex (STNR), Tonic Labyrinthine Reflex (TLR), and Spinal Galant Reflex (definitions of reflexes are in the end Glossary). For a more in-depth understanding, screening, and treatment options, please refer to a trained vision therapist.

The **visual perceptual skill** is the brain's ability to understand what the eyes see and interpret it appropriately, including depth, figure-ground (distinguishing objects from the background), location, visual closure (recognizing a familiar object when it is partially obscured), and more.

Visual acuity is the eye's ability to see clearly. Note that a person can have high visual acuity (i.e., 20/20 vision) and still have difficulty with visual perception.

Visual fixation is the eye's ability to maintain gaze on an object for an extended period of time. Visual fixation is the first critical skill to develop before more advanced visual skills. Once the eyes can fixate, they can learn to track a moving target. There are two visual tracking skills: smooth pursuit and saccade.

Image #3: Visual fixation and visual tracking

Binocular vision is the ability to move and use both eyes equally and effectively. When binocular vision is poor, it can cause disorders such as amblyopia (also known as "lazy eye" with one eye having less acuity) and strabismus (crossed or misaligned eye).

Saccade is the eye's ability to accurately jump back and forth between targets. **Smooth pursuit** is the eye's ability to smoothly and accurately track a moving object or line. For instance, while copying from a whiteboard, the eyes need to follow a straight line (*smooth pursuit*) to read what is on the board and look down quickly from the board to the paper without losing their place (*saccade*). Similarly, when we read our eyes follow a straight line (*smooth pursuit*) from left to right, then quickly jump to the second line of the first letter on the left side (*saccade*). During this process, both eyes have to cross the midline and work together.

AUDITORY SKILLS

Any reflex pattern that moves the head, including the ATNR, affects and influences auditory skills development. Auditory skill and perception are the brain's ability to focus on what is heard, process the information, and perceive and respond appropriately. This book will target auditory figure-ground, localization, binaural hearing, and receptive language.

Auditory figure-ground is the ability to hear specific sounds in a noisy environment. For example: your child will be able to respond to your call amid all the noise at the playground or while watching TV. **Auditory localization** is the ability to perceive and locate from where a sound is coming. For example: the child can turn toward the sound and locate the source.

Image #4: Child turns head toward a source of sound.

Binaural hearing is the ability to hear with both ears equally, and **receptive language** refers to the ability to understand and interpret sounds, words, and sentences accurately. For a more in-depth understanding, screening, and treatment options for receptive language and speech, please refer to a speech therapist.

VESTIBULAR SKILLS

The **vestibular system** is a sensory organ, located in the inner ear (see image below). It is located in both the right and left inner ears, and gives feedback to the brain regarding the head position, motion, balance, posture, and spatial relation. Similar to the visual and auditory system, any reflex pattern that moves the head, including the ATNR, affects the vestibular system.

Image #5: Location of the vestibular system

AN OVERVIEW OF THE BENEFITS OF THE ASYMMETRICAL TONIC NECK REFLEX (ATNR):

- assists with the birthing process;

- assists with reaching and exploration;

- influences auditory processing skills (hearing), such as depth, distance, localization, and figure-ground perception;

- assists with cross-lateral movements in early development, such as rolling, creeping, crawling, and walking;

- influences the visual skills (sight), such as depth perception, visual fixation, binocular vision, tracking, and more;

- helps with fine motor skills and eye-hand coordination;

- influences the vestibular system, which affects balance, spatial orientation, and posture;

- influences gross motor coordination;

- is critical for one-sided movement pattern and dominance (eye, ear, arm, and leg);

- assists with speech and language development;

- assists with overall motor coordination (movement);

- enables asymmetrical-sided motor coordination between our right and left brain, and our ability to cross the midline of the body and coordinate both parts of the body to perform a functional task (known as "right- and left-side discrimination"); and

- allows development of other reflexes, such as the Symmetrical Tonic Neck Reflex (STNR), also known as a learning reflex. The STNR contributes to the organization and perception of the binocular vision and binaural hearing.

C. RETAINED ASYMMETRICAL TONIC NECK REFLEX (ATNR): SIGNS, SYMPTOMS, AND BEHAVIORS

When the ATNR is active (retained) in the body past the integration stage, it creates a host of issues in the child's fine motor and gross motor development, auditory processing, visual, vestibular, focus, and attention skills.

SIGNS AND SYMPTOMS OF A RETAINED ASYMMETRICAL TONIC NECK REFLEX (ATNR)

Gross motor challenges, such as:

- difficulty rolling;

- difficulty crawling;

- lack of balance, instability;

- lack of coordination;

- challenges with crossing the midline;

- difficulty following multiple step movement instructions;

- problems and frustrations with sports;

- may appear clumsy (e.g., constantly dropping objects);

- mixed laterality: does not have a right- or left-side dominance (eye, ear, foot, and hand);

- the body might look robotic when running or crawling. Instead of the opposite arms and legs coordinating for a smooth movement pattern, the right arm and leg move together and vice versa (see Image #6).

Image #6: Robotic movement pattern: one-sided movement (e.g., right leg and arm move together and vice versa when running)

Image #7: Cross-lateral, oppositional movement; opposite sides moving in unison

Fine motor skills challenges, such as:

- challenges with eye-hand coordination;

- inability to coordinate both hands in unison to perform a task;

- handwriting difficulties:

  o presses hard on the paper, rips paper, and has difficulty erasing mistakes. Every time the child crosses the midline, there might be a slight opening of the hand. Most children accommodate by holding their pencil firmly and pressing hard, seldom breaking pencils.

  o hands cramp up and fatigue easily;

  o loses place on the page;

  o possibly develops an adverse behavioral reaction to handwriting;

- mixed laterality: no right- or left-side dominance (eye, ear, foot, and hand).

- Poor speech production

Visual skills challenges, such as:

- difficulty/challenges with binocular vision;

- difficulty with spelling and reading skills (e.g., Dyslexic tendencies);

- poor visual-motor skills (e.g., handwriting, dressing, feeding, etc.);

- poor ability to copy from paper or a whiteboard;

- difficulty with visual tracking; unable to follow a moving target;

- may complain of fatigue and losing place when reading;

- Dyscalculia (challenges with math).

Auditory skills challenges, such as:

- difficulty localizing sound; may have a hard time understanding from where a sound is coming;

- difficulty tuning out background sounds; easily distracted;

- difficulty following or remembering multiple verbal instructions; may pick up only the last one or two instructions and miss what was said first;

- appearing easily distracted or "tuned out."

Attention and concentration challenges, such as:

- poor speech and language development,

- difficulty with concentration and attention,

- lack of focus and attention (Attention Deficit Disorder (ADD) or Attention Deficit Hyperactivity Disorder (ADHD) tendencies).

CHAPTER 3

TESTING AND SCREENING

There are specific testing methods that trained therapists and service providers use to check for retained Asymmetrical Tonic Neck Reflex (ATNR). This book, however, is not designed to teach any one testing method. To learn more about testing as a teacher, refer to *Assessing Neuromotor Readiness for Learning: INPP Developmental Screening Test and School Intervention Programme*. Trained clinicians can consult *Neuromotor Immaturity in Children and Adults: The INPP Screening Test for Clinicians and Health Practitioners*.

While not a formal evaluation method, I have compiled a symptom and behavioral checklist (Table #1) to be filled out by parents and teachers during the screening process. This screening list should only be used to gather data, not to determine a specific diagnosis.

TABLE #1: SYMPTOMS AND BEHAVIORAL CHECKLIST: ASYMMETRICAL TONIC NECK REFLEX (ATNR)

Observe the child and circle the number that best represents the severity of the symptoms you observe. You can use this checklist first to gather data for an initial baseline and then again 6-12 weeks after the start of intervention to assess progress.

	Symptoms and Behaviors						
1	Difficulty with handwriting; holds a pencil very tightly or breaks pencils frequently (may complain of fatigue or hand cramps)	0	1	2	3	4	5
2	Challenges with reading skills (dyslexic tendencies)	0	1	2	3	4	5
3	Difficulty copying from a board; loses place, skips lines, or becomes confused	0	1	2	3	4	5
4	Difficulty following multi-step verbal instructions (e.g., only remembers the last step, looks confused, needs several repetitions, etc.)	0	1	2	3	4	5
5	Difficulty tuning out background sounds (e.g., needs several repetitions or face-to-face conversation; easily distracted)	0	1	2	3	4	5
6	Robotic running-movement pattern (i.e., right leg and arm move together and vice-versa when running)	0	1	2	3	4	5
7	Appears clumsy (e.g., frequently drops objects)	0	1	2	3	4	5
8	Difficulty with an activity of daily living, such as dressing, brushing teeth, tying shoes, etc.	0	1	2	3	4	5
9	Difficulty with ball games (e.g., catching, throwing, kicking, and hitting)	0	1	2	3	4	5
10	Difficulty with visual tracking skills (e.g., may skip a line when reading, complains of fatigue, confusion, etc.)	0	1	2	3	4	5

11	Difficulty with binocular visual skills (e.g., eyes not tracking at the same time, eyes turn, or wander away)	0	1	2	3	4	5
12	Poor handwriting skills (e.g., Dysgraphia [difficulty with spelling and putting thoughts in writing)	0	1	2	3	4	5
13	Mixed laterality (e.g., switches hands constantly when writing or uses both hands to stabilize pencil on paper)	0	1	2	3	4	5
14	Lack of one-side dominance (e.g., hand, foot, ear, or eye)	0	1	2	3	4	5
15	Difficulty locating from where a sound is coming	0	1	2	3	4	5
16	Poor balance and stability	0	1	2	3	4	5
17	Poor bilateral coordination	0	1	2	3	4	5
18	Difficulty crossing the midline (e.g., unable to imitate an activity which requires the body to cross over to the opposite side)	0	1	2	3	4	5
19	Poor speech and language skills	0	1	2	3	4	5
20	Difficulty with concentration and attention (e.g., may have ADD or ADHD tendencies)	0	1	2	3	4	5
21	Dyscalculia (difficulty with math)	0	1	2	3	4	5
22	Difficulty with skipping, jumping, and balancing games (e.g., hopscotch, jump rope, etc.)	0	1	2	3	4	5
23	Difficulty crawling or may have skipped the crawling milestone altogether	0	1	2	3	4	5

24	Difficulty and frustration playing sports	0	1	2	3	4	5
25	Difficulty following multiple-step movement instructions	0	1	2	3	4	5
26	May have had challenges with rolling during early childhood	0	1	2	3	4	5
27	May have difficulty with spelling and reading (dyslexic tendencies)	0	1	2	3	4	5
28	Difficulty with eye-foot coordination	0	1	2	3	4	5
29	Might appear easily distracted or "tuned out"	0	1	2	3	4	5
30	Poor handwriting skills (e.g., losing place while copying or not able to write on a straight line)	0	1	2	3	4	5

Table #1: Symptoms and Behavior Checklist for Asymmetrical Tonic Neck Reflex (ATNR)

Note: Usually, one retained reflex leads to the retention of other reflexes. To be safe, work on all of the primitive reflexes. Before working with a child, go through the symptoms checklist, and rate the severity of the symptoms or behaviors on a scale of 0-5, 0 being "not seen" to 5, being seen "all the time."

Visit https://ritp.info/atnr-book for downloadable version.

ADDITIONAL SCREENING

You can use the following exercises as part of the screening process **to determine if further testing is needed**. Inability to perform the following exercises well might be a sign of a retained ATNR.

SCREEN 1: STANDING HEAD TURN WITH STRAIGHT ARMS

1. Have the child stand up straight, and raise both arms in front of them to shoulder height.

2. Instruct the child to keep elbows straight as much as possible.

3. Stand behind the child and gently turn the head to the right.

4. Notice what the rest of the body does.

5. Ask the child to hold the head position for a few seconds while you observe.

6. Repeat on the other side.

GOAL

1. Elbows, shoulders, hips, and knees are able to remain straight while the head moves to one side.

OBSERVATION AND SIGNS OF ATNR RETENTION

☐ The elbow the head turns away from bends.

☐ The knee the head turns away from bends.

☐ The entire body moves with the direction of the head.

SCREEN 2: ZOMBIE MARCHING IN PLACE

1. Raise both arms to shoulder height with the head turned to the left, while marching in place.

2. Ask the child to keep arms and elbows straight as much as possible.

3. Repeat on the other side.

GOALS

1. Elbows are able to stay straight.

2. The child is able to lift both knees to the same height.

OBSERVATION AND SIGNS OF ATNR RETENTION

☐ Child has difficulty keeping the arms straight the entire time.

☐ The elbow the head turns away from bends.

☐ Child is unable to bring both knees up to the same height.

☐ The body shifts with the direction of the head.

SCREEN 3: HEAD TURNS ON ALL 4S

1. Have the child get down on all fours (hands and knees) with elbows straight, maintaining a "tabletop" position.

2. As much as possible, the child's head should be parallel to the floor and not dropping or extending so as not to trigger another reflex pattern.

3. Gently hold the child's head, and slightly turn it to the left or the right.

4. Observe the body, specifically the elbows.

5. Repeat on the other side.

GOALS

1. The child is able to move the head without moving any part of the body.

2. Elbows, shoulders, hips, and knees are able to remain still.

OBSERVATION AND SIGNS OF ATNR RETENTION

☐ The elbow the head turns away from bends.

☐ The entire body shifts or turns toward the direction of the head.

☐ The child is unable to maintain balance and stability.

Self-initiated head turn

Now, ask the child to keep the elbows as straight as possible while turning (self initiating) the head from side to side.

OBSERVATIONS

- Check to see if one side is more challenging than the other.

- Check if the child can self-correct when the body is moving.

CHAPTER 4

ADDRESSING A RETAINED ASYMMETRICAL TONIC NECK REFLEX (ATNR)

A. INTERVENTION AND TREATMENT PLANNING

The exercises compiled in this book are for those who are receiving occupational therapy or other reflex integration treatments. Use them as a daily home program and as movement breaks in a school setting with the help of a trained professional.

There are a number of interventions that may be appropriate for a child with a retained ATNR. One of the simplest ways to help integrate primitive reflexes is by mimicking early-childhood movement patterns.

Note: In addition to the gross and fine motor skills, the ATNR affects the auditory, visual, vestibular, and midline crossing skills. Working on the ATNR without triggering other reflexes is difficult, especially if the child has multiple reflexes retained. **To best serve the child, try the exercises from simple to hard before adding more challenging tasks that might frustrate them.**

To help incorporate auditory processing skills and responses, we will use cues such as clapping, snapping, counting, or the use of metronomes. A **metronome** is a device used by musicians that marks a tempo in beat-per-minute. You can use a physical metronome device or download a mobile app. The use of a metronome will increase the challenge of the exercise and, at the same time, help you focus more on the child and less on giving verbal cues. When choosing a tempo, if the child tends to go very fast, start with a faster tempo, and gradually slow it down. If the child tends to go very slowly, start with a slower tempo, and gradually increase the speed. Do not get frustrated. Meet children at their skill level.

Note: A proper visual processing skill is necessary for learning, and it is usually misdiagnosed. It is crucial to make sure a child is screened by a vision therapist to rule out possible retained reflexes and visual skill delays that may affect learning.

B. ACCOMMODATIONS

A child with a retained ATNR may have delayed verbal and visual responses. For a classroom or workstation, choose one or more of the following accommodations to meet the child's needs:

1. Position the child in front of the classroom board.

2. Place materials to copy on the child's desk to minimize head-turning during copying.

3. Break down verbal instruction:

    a. Provide written instruction for review.

    b. Have the child repeat the first instruction before adding additional instructions.

4. For movement activities, accommodate right- and left-side confusion by providing the following:

    a. visual cues to help differentiate the right and left sides of the body,

    b. a picture or video to imitate,

    c. a breakdown of the steps.

5. Provide movement breaks from the exercises described in this book to help promote ATNR integration.

6. Do not force games and sports; the child may not be ready for advanced movements without breaking down the steps.

7. If reading is difficult, try the following strategies:

    a. Have the child track letters with fingers.

    b. Use a ruler or visual cues under the line the child is reading.

    c. Cover all text except the line being read.

C. EXERCISES TO PROMOTE THE ASYMMETRICAL TONIC NECK REFLEX (ATNR)

The exercises below can be used in the order you think is best for your child. Follow the order presented here, or combine the exercises with others during your session. The manner in which you utilize the exercises depends on the environment, the child's state, and the materials you have on hand. For example, make the activities fun and exciting when working with younger children, but feel free to create more of a workout session with older children and adults. Avoid activities that create frustration and anxiety. As much as possible, try to make the exercises fun and enjoyable. For kids who are younger and refuse to cooperate, incorporate the use of positive reinforcement or rewards to encourage participation.

Note: The following exercises challenge more than one of the primitive reflexes, including the ATNR, encourage bilateral coordination, spatial awareness, visual skills, auditory skills, and motor planning skills. Do these games and activities during the child's therapy sessions, daily movement breaks, and home exercise program. I have added additional modifications and accommodations for exercises that many children find difficult. You can incorporate those steps, but they are not always necessary.

1) FISH

MATERIALS: Yoga Mat

1. Have the child lay down on their stomach, face to the mat, legs straight, elbow to shoulder height, and thumbs pointing toward the head.

2. Instruct the child to lift his head slightly, about 4-5 inches, and hold.

3. Push the floor with hands and forearms.

4. Hold for 3-5 seconds.

5. Bend and lift the right knee close to hip height.

6. Hold for 5 seconds.

7. Straighten the right leg, and slowly lower the head and upper body to the floor.

8. Repeat steps 2-4.

9. Bend and lift the left knee close to hip height.

10. Repeat 5-7 times.

VARIATION

1. Incorporate right and left knee lifts without lowering the head 7-10 times.

2. **Turn the head to the right and to the left** while maintaining lifted position.

3. Add metronome to work on auditory processing and timing.

GOALS

1. Complete smooth and controlled movement independently.

2. Bilateral coordination

3. Visual skills (peripheral vision)

4. Body awareness

5. Right- and left-side discrimination

6. Motor planning and timing

7. Auditory processing

POSITIVE SIGNS

- ☐ Uses fluid and controlled movements

- ☐ Capable of right- and left-side discrimination

- ☐ Able to sequence movements

- ☐ Able to bring head up independently

NEGATIVE SIGNS

- ☐ Unable to turn head without moving the arms

- ☐ Unable to sequence movements correctly

- ☐ Unable to isolate movements (e.g., arms and hands start to move sideways)

MODIFICATIONS

- ☐ Give a tactile cue by touching the leg that needs to move.

- ☐ Focus on one side before switching to the opposite side (e.g., do 3-5 rounds of one leg lift, rest, and then switch sides).

2) CRAWLING

MATERIALS: Tape

1. Tape a straight line on the floor.

2. Ask the child to get on all four hands and knees, and crawl following the line.

3. Have the child focus the gaze slightly forward while watching the line on the floor and not dropping the chin too low.

4. Have the child crawl, following the line.

VARIATIONS

☐ Use a metronome to work on auditory skills and timing.

☐ Crawl forward and backward with the same sides (i.e., right arm and right leg move together, and left arm and left leg move together).

☐ Crawl forward and backward contralaterally (i.e., right arm and left leg move together, and left arm and right leg move together).

GOALS

1. Bilateral coordination

2. Motor planning and timing

3. Crossing the midline

4. Spatial orientation

5. Visual skill (peripheral vision, visual fixation, visual tracking)

6. Body awareness

7. Right- and left-side discrimination

8. Shoulder stability and strength

9. Balance

10. Stability and strength

11. Auditory processing

POSITIVE SIGNS

- Able to motor plan and coordinate smooth movement patterns

- Understands and executes movement

- Able to keep the spine straight, not drooping or wiggling, and parallel with floor

- Able to crawl on a straight line

- Able to follow a metronome without frustration

NEGATIVE SIGNS

- Unable to crawl by following the line

- Unable to coordinate, balance, or keep the spine parallel to the floor

- Frustration with metronome and unable to slow down to match movement with sound

- Body wiggles around (e.g., side bending, squirmy, etc)

MODIFICATION

- Use visual cues to help a child with a motor plan. (e.g., place stickers on hands, colorful bands to match with legs, or colored placemats to step on).

3) CRAWLING WITH HEAD TURN

MATERIALS: Soft ball or soft toy

1. Start the child on all fours, with hands and knees on the floor in "tabletop" position, and the head in a straight line with the spine.

2. Have the child turn the head to the right, and hold a soft beanbag or a soft toy between the chin and shoulder.

3. While maintaining the hold, ask the child to crawl forward and backward for 10 feet.

4. Repeat on the left side.

Note: The ball is a tactile cue to help the child maintain the position. Once the child is able to do the exercises with the ball under the chin, practice doing the exercise without it. Also, since crawling exercises also target additional reflexes, such as the Symmetrical Tonic Neck and Spinal Galant Reflexes, address those reflexes if crawling is a challenge.

VARIATIONS

- If you are not using a ball as a tactile cue, use an image the child can visually track on the wall.

- Add the use of metronome to work on timing and auditory processing.

GOALS

1. Complete smooth and controlled movement independently

2. Bilateral coordination

3. Visual skill (peripheral vision, visual fixation, and visual tracking)

4. Body awareness

5. Right- and left-side discrimination

6. Auditory processing

7. Crossing the midline

POSITIVE SIGNS

- [ ] Able to maintain a head turn while crawling backward and forward

- [ ] Able to crawl on a line (path marked out)

- [ ] Able to maintain straight elbows

NEGATIVE SIGNS

- [ ] Drops the ball

- [ ] The head begins to straighten while crawling

- [ ] The elbow the head turned away from bends and cannot remain straight

- [ ] Unable to hold a head turn with straight elbow

- [ ] Difficulty crawling on a straight line

4) SOLDIER CRAWL (SPIDERMAN CRAWL)

MATERIALS: None

1. Have the child lay flat on the floor.

2. Lift the right arm and the left leg; move forward while the opposite arm and leg stabilize the body.

3. Pull yourself forward and simultaneously shift weight to the left.

4. Lift the left arm and the right leg; move them forward while the opposite arm and leg stabilize the body.

5. Pull yourself forward, and simultaneously shift weight to the right.

6. Crawl forward 15-20 feet.

VARIATION

1. Use metronome to work on auditory processing and timing.

GOALS

1. Bilateral coordination

2. Motor planning and timing

3. Crossing the midline

4. Spatial orientation

5. Visual skill (peripheral vision, visual fixation, visual tracking)

6. Body awareness

7. Right- and left-side discrimination

8. Posture and balance

9. Stability and strength

10. Auditory processing

POSITIVE SIGNS

☐ Smooth and coordinated movement pattern

☐ All four limbs coordinate simultaneously; no lagging

☐ Able to time movement with metronome

NEGATIVE SIGNS

- ☐ Unable to coordinate

- ☐ Not using one side of the body (e.g. prefers to move using one side of the body and neglects the other)

- ☐ Difficulty differentiating right and left sides of the body

- ☐ Confusion and frustration

- ☐ Drags body on the floor instead of coordinating movement properly

- ☐ Difficulty timing movement with metronome

MODIFICATIONS

- ☐ Give physical cues by either placing the correct arm and leg on the floor or tapping (touching) the side that needs to move.

- ☐ Use verbal cues: verbally cue the child what to do.

- ☐ Visual cues: use visual cues to help a child motor plan (e.g., use stickers on hands and place the same colored sticker on the opposite leg that needs to move in unison. Ask the child to move only the same colored stickers.

- ☐ Have the child crawl on knees and hands.

5) WALL PUSH-UPS

MATERIALS: None

1. Have the child stand in front of a wall, with both hands flat on the wall and parallel to each other.

2. While hands are on the wall, ask the child to step back, far enough to keep elbows straight and increase weight on the arms, so at least 20% of the weight is supported with the hands.

3. Practice wall push-ups. Have the child bend elbows while facing the wall.

4. Ask the child to turn the head to the left, and complete 3-5 wall push-ups while maintaining the head turn.

5. Next, have the child turn the head to the right, and complete 3-5 wall push-ups.

VARIATION

1. Add metronome to work on auditory processing and timing.

GOALS

1. Complete smooth and controlled movement independently

2. Bilateral coordination

3. Visual skill (peripheral vision, visual fixation)

4. Body awareness

5. Right- and left-side discrimination

6. Strength and stability

7. Auditory processing

POSITIVE SIGNS

- [ ] Able to maintain head turn during push-ups

- [ ] Both elbows move in unison regardless the direction the head turned

NEGATIVE SIGNS

- [ ] The opposite elbow the head turned away from bends

- [ ] Unable to move both elbows in unison

- [ ] Collapsing on one side

- [ ] Unable to maintain a head turn during wall push-up

MODIFICATION

☐ Hold a wall plank with the head turned for approximately 10 seconds on each side

6) ROLLING ON A STRAIGHT LINE

MATERIALS: Floor space for rolling; a visual straight line marked on the floor

1. Have the child lay down on the floor with the shoulder on top of the line.

2. Ask the child to roll while keeping the shoulders on the line.

3. If shoulders are not on the line, ask the child to adjust self before rolling over again.

4. Roll back in the opposite direction.

GOALS

1. Bilateral coordination

2. Motor planning and timing

3. Visual perception, tracking, scanning, and peripheral vision

4. Body awareness

5. Right- and left-side discrimination

6. Crossing the midline

7. Gross motor skills

8. Spatial orientation

POSITIVE SIGNS

☐ Able to roll on a straight line on either side

☐ Able to independently fix body position when not on line

NEGATIVE SIGNS

☐ Difficulty aligning self on a straight line while rolling

☐ Awkward movement pattern

7) HINGE

MATERIALS: Yoga Mat

1. Have the child lay down on their back with legs and arms straight, chin perpendicular to the floor, and eyes looking at the ceiling.

2. Ask the child to turn the head to the right and simultaneously do the following:

   a. Bend and lift the right knee while leaving feet flat on the floor.

   b. Bend and slide the right elbow on the floor until it reaches the right shoulder.

   c. Track the right hand with the eyes as it moves.

3. Hold for 3-5 seconds.

4. Return the body to Step 1 while tracking the movement of the right hand with eyes.

5. Ask the child to turn the head to the left while simultaneously:

   a. Bend and lift the left knee while leaving feet flat on the floor

   b. Bend and slide the left elbow on the floor until it reaches the left shoulder

   c. Track the left hand with the eyes as it moves.

6. Hold for 3-5 seconds.

7. Repeat 5-7 times.

VARIATION

Once the child can perform the above exercise well, try the following variation:

1. Ask the child to close their eyes and follow verbal cues only (focus on auditory processing and proprioception).

2. Alternate between the right and left sides, without a pause, 7-10 times.

3. Use a metronome to mark movement through the steps.

*When choosing a tempo, if the child tends to go very fast, start with a faster tempo and gradually slow it down. If the child tends to go very slowly, start with a slower tempo, and gradually increase the speed. Do not be frustrated. Meet them at their skill level.

GOALS

1. Complete smooth and controlled movement independently

2. Bilateral coordination

3. Visual skill (peripheral vision, visual fixation, and visual tracking)

4. Body awareness

5. Right- and left-side discrimination

6. Auditory processing

POSITIVE SIGNS

- ☐ Fluid and controlled movement

- ☐ Good body awareness (right- and left-side discrimination)

- ☐ Able to sequence the arm and leg in unison

- ☐ Able to visually track the moving hand

- ☐ Able to keep the opposite side of the body still

- ☐ Able to sequence movement with only auditory instruction

NEGATIVE SIGNS

- ☐ Unable to sequence the arm and leg in unison

- ☐ Confusion and distraction

- ☐ Consistently misses a step and requires additional cues to correct

- ☐ One side moves faster than the other

- ☐ Unable to sequence movements correctly

- ☐ Delayed response

- ☐ The opposite arm and/or leg moves

MODIFICATIONS

☐ Break down the exercise by either focusing on the arm or the leg.

☐ Give verbal cues to help correct mistakes.

☐ Give tactile cues (touch) to guide the child to move the correct arms and legs.

8) LIZARD 1

MATERIALS: Yoga Mat

1. Have the child lay down on their stomach, face to the mat, with straight arms and legs.

2. Ask the child to turn their head to the right while simultaneously doing the following:

   a. Sliding the right arm up, until the elbows reach shoulder height.

   b. Sliding the right leg up, knees bent but not passing hip height.

3. Hold for 3-5 seconds.

4. Return to Step 1, the starting position.

5. Ask the child to turn head to the left while simultaneously:

a. Sliding the left arm up, until the elbows reach shoulder height.

b. Sliding the left leg up, knees bent but not passing hip height.

6.   Hold for 3-5 seconds.

7.   Repeat steps 1-6 up to 7-10 times.

VARIATIONS

*Once the child can perform the exercise well, try the following:

1. Ask the child to close their eyes and follow only verbal cues (auditory processing and proprioception).

2. Alternate turns between right and left sides, without a pause, 7-10 times.

3. Use a metronome to mark movement through the steps.

*When choosing a tempo, if the child tends to go very fast, start with a faster tempo and gradually slow it down. If the child tends to go very slowly, start with a slower tempo, and gradually increase the speed. Do not get frustrated. Meet them at their skill level.

GOALS

1. Complete smooth and controlled movement independently

2. Bilateral coordination

3. Visual skills (peripheral vision, visual fixation, and visual tracking)

4. Body awareness

5. Right- and left-side discrimination

6. Auditory processing

POSITIVE SIGNS

☐ Fluid and controlled movement

☐ Good body awareness (right- and left-side discrimination)

☐ Able to sequence the arm and leg in unison

☐ Able to keep the opposite side of the body still

☐ Able to sequence movement with auditory instruction only

NEGATIVE SIGNS

☐ Unable to sequence the arm and leg in unison

☐ Confusion and distraction

☐ Consistently misses a step and requires additional cues to correct

☐ One side moves faster than the other

☐ Unable to sequence movements correctly

☐ Delayed response

☐ The opposite arm and/or leg moves

MODIFICATIONS

☐ Break down the exercise by either focusing on the arm or the leg.

☐ Give verbal cues to help correct mistakes.

☐ Give tactile cues (touch) to guide the child to move the correct arms and legs.

9) LIZARD 2

MATERIALS: Yoga Mat

1. Have the child lay down on their stomach, face to the mat, with elbows and shoulders at 90 degrees, hands flat, thumbs pointing to head and legs straight.

2. Ask the child to turn head to the right while simultaneously:

a. sliding right elbow to right hip, AND

b. sliding right knee to right elbow.

3. Hold the position for 3-5 seconds.

4. Return to starting position, Step 1.

5. Ask the child to turn head to the left while simultaneously:

    a. sliding left elbow to left hip, AND

    b. sliding left knee to left elbow.

6. Hold the position for 3-5 seconds.

7. Repeat steps 1-6, up to 7-10 times.

VARIATIONS

*Once the child can perform the exercise well, try the following:

1. Ask the child to close the eyes and follow verbal cues only (focus on auditory processing and proprioception).

2. Alternate turns between the right and left sides, without a pause, 7-10 times.

3. Use a metronome to mark movement through the steps.

*If the child tends to move fast, start with a faster tempo and gradually slow it down. If the child tends to move slowly, start with a slower tempo, and gradually increase the speed. Do not get frustrated! Aim to meet the child at his/her skill level. Importantly, this exercise triggers other reflexes, such as the Spinal Galant Reflex. If this exercise is a challenge, make sure to also work on the Spinal Galant Reflex and any other reflex that will support the child's development.

GOALS

1. Able to complete smooth and controlled movement independently

2. Bilateral coordination

3. Visual skill (peripheral vision, visual fixation, and visual tracking)

4. Body awareness

5. Right- and left-side discrimination

6. Auditory processing

POSITIVE SIGNS

☐ Fluid and controlled movement

☐ Good body awareness (right- and left-side discrimination)

☐ Able to sequence the arm and leg in unison

☐ Able to keep the opposite side of the body still

☐ Able to sequence movement with auditory instruction only

NEGATIVE SIGNS

- Unable to sequence the arm and leg in unison

- Confusion and distraction

- Consistently misses a step and requires additional cues to correct

- One side moves faster than the other

- Unable to sequence movements correctly

- Delayed response

- The opposite arm and leg move

- Side-bending

- Straightening of the arms and legs the head turned toward

MODIFICATION

- Focus only on the arms or the legs.

- Give verbal cues to help correct mistakes.

- Give tactile cues (touch) to guide the child to move the correct arms and legs.

10) PLANK WITH HEAD TURNS

MATERIALS: Yoga Mat

1. Have the child hold a full-body plank.

2. Ask the child to turn head to the left, and hold the plank for 3-5 seconds.

3. Take a break if necessary.

4. Ask the child to turn the head to the right, and hold the plank for 3-5 seconds.

5. Repeat 3-5 times.

VARIATIONS

1. Full push-ups with head turns

2. Knee push-up with head turns

3. Add metronome to work on auditory processing and timing

GOALS

1. Right- and left-side discrimination

2. Upper and lower body strength and stability

3. Strengthening of the hands

4. Auditory processing

5. Complete smooth and controlled movement independently

6. Bilateral coordination

7. Visual skill (peripheral vision, visual fixation)

8. Body awareness

POSITIVE SIGNS

☐ Able to maintain head turn with straight elbow

☐ Able to isolate head movements from body

NEGATIVE SIGNS

- [ ] The elbow the head turned away from bends automatically

- [ ] Unable to straighten the elbow the head turned away from

- [ ] Unable to maintain head turn; head begins to straighten up

- [ ] Knee or hip flexion (bending) and/or body twisting

MODIFICATION

- [ ] Plank on knees with head turn

- [ ] Wall Push-Ups, (Exercise #5)

11) RIGHT HAND WALL PUSH-UP
WITH HEAD-TURN

MATERIALS: Wall space

PREPARATION

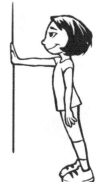

1. Child is able to do Exercise #5.

2. Have the child stand in front of a wall, with the right hand flat on the wall, at shoulder height.

3. While the right hand is on the wall, ask the child to turn the head to the right and to the left, while maintaining a straight elbow.

EXERCISE

1. While maintaining the left head turn, ask the child to do 1-3 right-handed wall push-ups.

2. Turn the head to the right, and do 1-3 right-handed push-ups.

3. Repeat 1-3 times.

VARIATIONS

1. Right-handed plank with head turn

2. Right-handed full push-up with head turn (Advanced)

3. Right-handed plank on knees with head turn

4. Right-handed push-up on knees with head turn (Advanced)

5. Plank with Rotation (see #16)

GOALS

1. Bilateral coordination

2. Visual skills (peripheral vision, visual fixation)

3. Body awareness

4. Right- and left-side discrimination

5. Upper- and lower-body strength and stability

6. Shoulder stability

7. Hand strengthening

8. Core strength and stability

POSITIVE SIGNS

☐ Able to maintain head turn during wall push-ups

☐ Able to maintain straight elbow during head turns

NEGATIVE SIGNS

☐ The elbow opposite the side the head turns toward bends when the head turns

☐ Unable to maintain head turn during wall push-up; head begins to straighten

☐ Unable to push up without straightening the head

☐ Elbow may buckle and the child loses balance

☐ Unable to keep feet still; fidgety and moving around

☐ Knee or hip flexion (bending) and/or body twisting

MODIFICATION

☐ Right-hand wall plank with head turn for 10-15 seconds at a time

☐ Wall Push-Ups, (Exercise #5)

12) LEFT-HAND WALL PUSH-UP WITH HEAD TURN

MATERIALS: Wall space

PREPARATION

1. Child is able to do Exercise #5.

2. Have the child stand in front of a wall, with the left hand flat on the wall, at shoulder height.

3. While the left hand is on the wall, ask the child to turn the head to the right and to the left, while maintaining a straight elbow.

EXERCISE

1. While maintaining the left head turn, ask the child to do 1-3 left-handed wall push-ups.

2. Turn the head to the right, and do 1-3 left-handed push-ups.

3. Repeat 1-3 times.

VARIATIONS

1. Left-handed plank with head turn

2. Left-handed full push-up with head turn (Advanced)

3. Left-handed plank on knees with head turn

4. Left-handed push-up on knees with head turn (Advanced)

GOALS

1. Bilateral coordination

2. Visual skill (peripheral vision, visual fixation)

3. Body awareness

4. Right- and left-side discrimination

5. Upper- and lower-body strength and stability

6. Shoulder stability

7. Hand strengthening

8. Core strength and stability

POSITIVE SIGNS

☐ Able to maintain head turn during wall push-ups

☐ Able to maintain straight elbow during head turns

NEGATIVE SIGNS

☐ The elbow immediately buckles when the head turns

☐ Unable to maintain head turn during wall push-up; head begins to straighten

☐ Unable to push up without straightening the head

☐ Elbow may buckle, and child loses balance or falls to the side

☐ Unable to keep feet still; fidgety and moving around

☐ Knee or hip flexion (bending) and/or body twisting

MODIFICATION

- [ ] Left-hand wall plank with head turn for 10-15 seconds at a time

- [ ] Wall Push-Ups, (Exercise #5)

13) CROSS PUSH WITH ONE HAND

MATERIALS: None

1. Stand facing your child.

2. Have the child raise his arms to shoulder height or a little lower with elbows straight.

3. Ask the child to raise the right arm and cross the midline to push your right hand.

4. Provide slight resistance to the child's hands with your right hand.

5. Ask the child to turn head to the left, while pushing your hand with the right hand.

6. Hold for 5-7 seconds.

7. Turn the head to the right while maintaining resistance.

8. Hold for 5-7 seconds.

9. Repeat 3-5 times.

10. Switch hands and repeat the exercise on the opposite side.

GOALS

1. Right- and left-side discrimination

2. Bilateral coordination

3. Motor planning and timing

4. Crossing the midline

5. Spatial orientation

6. Visual skill (peripheral vision, visual fixation, visual tracking)

7. Body awareness

8. Shoulder stability and strength

POSITIVE SIGNS

- ☐ Able to move head to one side without any changes to the body

- ☐ Able to maintain equal resistance with both arms

- ☐ Able to maintain equal resistance with both right and left hands

- ☐ Able to maintain elbow extension

NEGATIVE SIGNS

- ☐ Unable to independently cross arms

- ☐ Difficulty maintaining straight arms

- ☐ Knee or hip flexion (bending) and/or body twisting

- ☐ Twisting of the entire body

- ☐ Unable to isolate the head movement from the rest of the body

MODIFICATION

- ☐ If crossing the arm is difficult, continue practicing one-handed wall push-up.

14) CROSS PUSH WITH BOTH HANDS

MATERIALS: None

1. Stand facing your child.

2. Have the child raise his arms to shoulder height or a little lower with elbows straight.

3. Ask the child to cross his arms with the right arm on top of the left arm, maintaining a straight elbow.

4. Place your right hand on the child's right hand, and your left hand on the child's left hand, and give resistance.

5. While maintaining straight elbows and resistance in both arms, ask the child to turn head to the left.

6. Hold for 5-7 seconds.

7. Ask the child to turn head to the right and hold for another 5-7 seconds.

8. Repeat 3-5 times.

Switch Hands

1. Do the same on the opposite side, but first have the child cross arms with the left arm on top of the right arm.

2. While maintaining straight elbows and resistance in both hands, ask the child to turn the head to the right.

3. Hold for 5-7 seconds.

4. Ask the child to turn head to the left, and hold for another 5-7 seconds.

5. Repeat 3-5 times.

GOALS

1. Bilateral coordination

2. Motor planning and timing

3. Crossing the midline

4. Spatial orientation

5. Visual skill (peripheral vision, visual fixation, visual tracking)

6. Body awareness

7. Right- and left-side discrimination

8. Shoulder stability and strength

POSITIVE SIGNS

☐ Able to move head to one side without any changes to the body

☐ Able to maintain equal resistance with both arms

☐ Able to maintain equal resistance with both right and left hands

☐ Able to maintain elbow extension

NEGATIVE SIGNS

☐ Unable to independently cross arms

☐ Difficulty maintaining straight arms

☐ Knee or hip flexion (bending) and/or body twisting

☐ Entire body may twist

☐ Unable to isolate the head movement from the rest of the body

MODIFICATIONS

☐ Practice exercise sitting down.

☐ If crossing both arms becomes difficult, continue to practice one arm at a time.

15) ZOMBIE MARCH

MATERIALS: None

1. Have the child stand straight and raise arms to shoulder height

2. Check if the child is able to keep elbows straight when turning head from side to side. (If this stage is difficult, keep practicing before moving to the next step)

3. Ask the child to keep arms and elbows straight, while turning head to the left and marching 10 steps.

4.   Turn head to the right, and march 10 steps.

VARIATIONS

1.   Use metronomes to incorporate auditory processing.

2.   March forward and backward, while taping right knee with right hand, and left knee with left hand (same sides).

3.   March with hands raised to the side at shoulder height.

4.   Add hand weights and/or ankle weights.

GOALS

1.   Bilateral coordination

2.   Motor planning and timing

3.   Crossing the midline

4.   Spatial orientation

5. Visual skills (peripheral vision, visual fixation, visual tracking)

6. Body awareness

7. Right- and left-side discrimination

8. Posture and balance

9. Core stability and strength

10. Upper-body strength

11. Shoulder stability

12. Auditory processing

POSITIVE SIGNS

☐ Smooth and coordinated movement pattern

☐ Able to keep both elbows straight during marching

☐ Able to time movement with metronome

☐ Able to lift both knees up to same height

NEGATIVE SIGNS

☐ Unable to coordinate movement

☐ Head starts to straighten when marching

☐ The elbow the head turned away from starts to bend

☐ Difficulty timing movement with metronome

MODIFICATIONS

☐ Practice head turns with raised arms and straight elbows without the march

☐ Seated position, and march by lifting feet off the ground (straight arms and turned head).

☐ Give physical or verbal cues to keep elbows straight.

16) PLANK WITH ROTATION

MATERIALS: Yoga mat

This exercise requires core strength. Consider it only for older kids and adults.

1. Start with a full plank (hands and feet on the floor).

2. Ask the child to lift the right arm, and rotate body until both arms and body are in the same line.

3. Maintain eye gaze on the right hand.

4. Hold for 3-5 seconds.

5. Return to starting position.

6. Lift the left arm, and rotate it to the left until both arms and the body are in the same line.

7. Hold for 3-5 seconds.

GOALS

1. Bilateral coordination

2. Motor planning and timing

3. Balance

4. Spatial orientation

5. Visual skill (peripheral vision, visual fixation, visual tracking)

6. Body awareness

7. Right- and left-side discrimination

8. Shoulder stability and strength

9. Core stability

POSITIVE SIGNS

- Maintaining proper posture and strength on both sides of the body

- Able to maintain eye gaze on the moving hand while keeping the opposite elbow straight

- Able to keep the opposite leg straight while the body is rotating

- Able to maintain straight elbow on the weight-bearing arm

NEGATIVE SIGNS

- Unable to maintain head turn during rotation

- Unable to keep opposite leg straight while the body is rotating

- Elbow buckles and body loses balance

- Unable to visually follow raised arm

MODIFICATIONS

- Practice lifting one hand from the floor a few inches to build arm, shoulder, and core strength

- Half-plank (knees on the floor)

- Plan with Head Turns (Exercise #10)

17) DRAW, WRITE, & COLOR ON THE GROUND ON ALL FOURS

MATERIALS: Chalk and surface on which to draw

1. While on hands and knees, have the child draw by crossing the midline.

2. Have the child look for specific letters, pictures, or shapes.

GOALS

1. Visual skills (peripheral vision, visual fixation, visual tracking)

2. Body awareness

3. Right- and left-side discrimination

4. Bilateral coordination

5. Gross motor development

6. Fine motor development

7. Upper-body strength

POSITIVE SIGNS

- ☐ Able to cross the midline without difficulty

- ☐ Able to move head from left to right with weight on one hand, while keeping elbow straight

- ☐ Smooth and fluid movements from side to side

- ☐ Able to stay on all fours while tracing and moving head from side to side

NEGATIVE SIGNS

- ☐ Right- or left-side neglect: child may make the majority of the marks, read, or scan on one side

- ☐ Difficulty crossing the midline

- ☐ Child might want to sit

- ☐ Weak upper-body strength

*Hand dominance might affect quality; however, the child should easily be able to make an arc and cross the midline similarly on both sides.

I have done this activity with a variety of media. Pick the one that works best for you. The main thing is for the child to have their weight on one hand while tracking and moving their head from side to side.

The aim is to strengthen and integrate the side that is weight bearing.

SUGGESTED MATERIALS:

- Construction paper and crayons or markers

- Chalk on concrete

- Vibrating pens to give extra proprioceptive input

- Finger paints (try having the child play with these during bath time)

- Be creative!

18) PRE-WRITING:
PAINT OR DRAW WHILE STANDING

MATERIALS: Paint brushes with paint or dry erase markers, vertical easel or dry erase board

1. Have the child face the drawing surface with paints or dry erase markers.

2. If needed, have a visual mark on the floor for the child to stand on.

3. Encourage the child to make large lines, arcs, circles, swirls, etc., while crossing the midline.

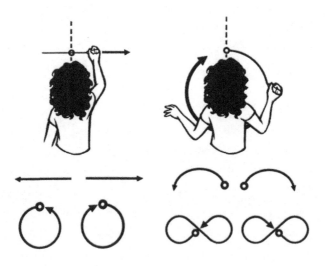

4. Repeat with the other hand.

GOALS

1. Visual skills (peripheral vision, visual fixation, visual tracking)

2. Body awareness

3. Right- and left-side discrimination

4. Bilateral coordination

5. Gross motor development

6. Fine motor development

7. Shoulder strength and stability

POSITIVE SIGNS

☐ Smooth and fluid movements from side to side

☐ Able to visually track from left to right

☐ Able to cross the midline without difficulty

☐ Able to move head from left to right without moving feet

NEGATIVE SIGNS

☐ Loss of balance

☐ Difficulty with visual tracking

☐ Walks or steps to draw; unable to keep feet stationary

☐ Right- or left-side neglect; child may make majority of the marks on one side

☐ Difficulty crossing midline

*Hand dominance might affect quality; however, the child should easily be able to make an arc and cross the midline similarly on both sides.

ADVANCED BILATERAL COORDINATION

MATERIALS: Paint brushes with paint or dry erase markers, vertical easel or dry erase board

1. Ask the child to use both hands to draw similar pre-writing symbols.

VARIATIONS

1. Vertical lines going up and down

2. Horizontal lines going to the right and to the left, and vice versa

3. Curves and circles

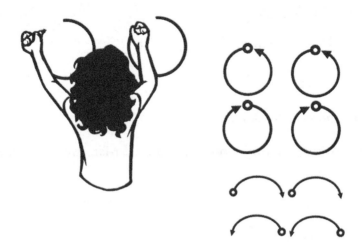

4. Infinity symbols

GOALS

1. Fine motor development

2. Crossing the midline

3. Eye-hand coordination

4. Upper-body strength

5. Motor planning

6. Right- and left-side discrimination

7. Posture

8. Gross motor development

9. Visual tracking: smooth pursuit, near-far, eye teaming, and saccade

POSITIVE SIGNS

☐ Able to trace and form pre-writing symbols by crossing the midline

☐ Able to keep straight elbows when arms move in any direction

☐ Able to cross the midline easily

NEGATIVE SIGNS

☐ Unable to trace or form pre-writing shapes by crossing the midline

☐ Unable to keep the elbow straight

☐ Difficulty with direction

☐ Extra difficulty with diagonal and infinity symbols

MODIFICATION

- ☐ Place a visual marker on the floor for the child to stand on

- ☐ Follow the developmental visual-motor development (i.e., vertica, horizontal, circle, cross, diagonal, and infinity)

19) COPYING FROM BOARD

If you suspect your child has visual skills deficiency, you should first consult with a vision therapist. The following supplemental worksheets are best used with the support of a vision therapist. You can use a variety of templates that are age- and grade-appropriate for your child. *Visit https://ritp.info/atnr-book to download supplemental worksheets.*

MATERIALS: Table, chair, pencil, worksheet, and wall space

- Place the visual tracking worksheet on the wall in front of the child.

- Have the child sit with proper posture in front of the wall.

- Ask the child to complete the worksheets.

GOALS

1. Hand-eye coordination

2. Visual skills: saccade, visual tracking, smooth pursuit

3. Fine motor development

4. Reading skills

5. Copying from a board

6. Handwriting skills

7. Improved posture

8. Focus and concentration

POSITIVE SIGNS

☐ Able to track and find their place easily

☐ Able to copy from a board

☐ Able to copy letters and symbols without skipping or missing a line

☐ Able to look up and down without losing their place

☐ Able to maintain a proper sitting posture

NEGATIVE SIGNS

☐ Unable to copy from a board

☐ Confusion

☐ Skips a line

- Skips letters or symbols

- Difficulty writing on a straight line

- Presses hard on paper to help stabilize hand from moving

- Difficulty maintaining a proper sitting posture

- Difficulty finding the next line

- Confusion and frustration

- Complaints and refusal to read or write

VARIATIONS

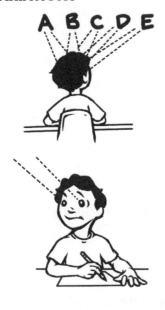

1. Place the worksheet directly in front of the child.

2. Place the worksheet in the right visual field.

3. Place the worksheet in the left visual field.

2O) VISUAL TRACKING (THUMB)

MATERIALS: Sticker or a small object the child can hold

1. Have the child stand with the right arm straight forward and the thumb up.

2. Ask the child to track the thumb with the eyes, without moving the head, 3-5 times horizontally.

3. Rest/Close the eyes for a rest, and repeat with the opposite arm.

4. Have the child stand with the right arm straight forward and the thumb up.

5. Ask the child to track the thumb with the eyes, without moving the head, 3-5 times in the following directions:

    a. horizontally

b.   diagonally

c.   circular motion

d.   infinity symbol

6.   Rest the eyes.

7.   Repeat using the left thumb.

GOALS

1. Visual tracking: smooth pursuit, eye teaming, and saccade

2. Crossing the midline

3. Hand-eye coordination

4. Upper-body strength

5. Body awareness

6. Posture

POSITIVE SIGNS

☐ Able to track from left to right following smooth eye movement without the eyes jumping back and forth

☐ Able to keep the head straight and move only the eyes while tracking the thumb with the eyes

☐ Able to keep the body straight and move the arm to the left and the right with a straight elbow

NEGATIVE SIGNS

☐ The head moves with the arm

☐ Unable to track thumb without the eyes jumping back and forth

☐ The child seems confused with the exercise

☐ Difficulty keeping the elbow straight when moving it from side to side

☐ The entire body turns with the arm

ADDITIONAL GAME IDEAS

- ☐ Near and far exercises are great for working on convergence and divergence of the eyes.

- ☐ Hold or post a cue card to copy farther away from the child.

- ☐ Use matching games and "I Spy."

MODIFICATIONS

- ☐ Seated visual tracking: have the child sit on a chair with back and shoulder support while visually tracking the thumb.

- ☐ Have the child track a small object you are holding.

- ☐ Repeat horizontal tracking before moving to tracking circles, diagonal lines, and infinity.

21) JUMPING JACKS

MATERIALS: None

1. Stand with legs straight and both arms at the side.

2. Jump and spread both legs open and arms over the head or shoulder height.

3. Jump and go back to the starting position.

4. Repeat 10 times.

VARIATION

1. Add metronome to work on auditory processing and timing.

GOALS

1. Motor planning and timing

2. Visual skills (peripheral vision, visual fixation, visual tracking)

3. Body awareness

4. Right- and left-side discrimination

5. Bilateral coordination

6. Balance

7. Strength and posture

8. Auditory processing

POSITIVE SIGNS

☐ Able to move arms and legs at the same time

☐ Able to coordinate and balance self

☐ Upright posture

NEGATIVE SIGNS

☐ Confusion

☐ Inability to coordinate movement

☐ Moves arms but not legs or vice versa

MODIFICATIONS

- ☐ Use visual cues to help the child initiate movements.

- ☐ Draw the steps and have the child follow them.

- ☐ Use verbal cues.

- ☐ Visually model the movement, and have the child imitate you.

- ☐ Focus on just the legs or the arms following verbal cues (e.g., metronome).

- ☐ Focus on one side at a time (e.g., step to the right and lift the right arm to the side).

22) CROSS CRAWLS (CROSS-LATERAL)

MATERIALS: None

1. Start from a standing position.

2. Ask the child to tap the right knee with the left hand, and the left knee with the right hand (opposite sides).

3. Repeat 10 times.

VARIATIONS

1. March forward and backward while tapping right knee with left hand, and left knee with right hand (opposite sides).

2. Tap the **left knee with the right elbow** and the **right knee with the left elbow**.

3. Reach back and tap the right ankle with the left hand, and the left ankle with the right hand.

4. Create a variety of combinations to work on motor planning and coordination.

5. Add metronome to work on auditory processing and timing.

GOALS

1. Bilateral coordination

2. Motor planning and timing

3. Crossing the midline

4. Spatial orientation

5. Visual skill (peripheral vision, visual fixation, visual tracking)

6. Body awareness

7. Right- and left-side discrimination

8. Posture and balance

9. Core stability and strength

10. Auditory processing

POSITIVE SIGNS

☐ Able to motor plan and coordinate smooth movement pattern

☐ Understands and executes movement independently

☐ Differentiates right and left sides of the body

☐ Maintains balance and upright posture

NEGATIVE SIGNS

☐ Confusion and frustration

☐ Unable to coordinate and execute movement

☐ Loses balance

☐ Difficulty timing metronome (auditory) and movement

☐ Taps same side instead of opposite side

MODIFICATIONS

☐ Seated cross crawl: do the same exercise while seated instead of standing.

☐ Use visual cues to help a child motor plan (e.g., use matching stickers on hands and knees/ankles.

☐ Breakdown steps and focus on one side at a time.

☐ Model the movement while the child imitates you.

23) PLANK SOLDIER CRAWL

MATERIALS: None

Note: Plank Soldier Crawl is an advanced exercise that requires core and upper body strength and shoulder stability and challenges multiple primitive reflexes. Best for older kids and adults.

1. Have the child lay flat on the floor.

2. Lift to plank with elbows and knees straight, with only hands and curled toes touching the floor.

3. Move forward by lifting and moving right arm and left leg, while the opposite arm and leg stabilize the body.

4. Stabilize.

5. Lift left arm and right leg, and move them forward.

6. Crawl forward up to 5 steps.

7. Rest.

8. Crawl backward up to 5 steps.

VARIATIONS

1. Use metronome to work on auditory processing and timing.

2. Alternate between elbows and hands, without the crawl, up to 5-10 times.

GOALS

1. Core stability and strength

2. Bilateral coordination

3. Motor planning and timing

4. Spatial orientation

5. Visual skills (peripheral vision, visual fixation, visual tracking)

6. Body awareness

7. Right- and left-side discrimination

8. Posture and balance

9. Auditory processing

POSITIVE SIGNS

☐ Smooth and coordinated movement pattern

☐ All four limbs coordinate simultaneously; no lagging

☐ Able to time movement with metronome

NEGATIVE SIGNS

☐ Unable to coordinate

☐ Unable to maintain posture; falls

☐ Unable to keep elbows straight

☐ Unable to keep knees straight; they may keep bending

☐ Difficulty differentiating right and left sides of the body

☐ Drags body on the floor instead of coordinating properly

☐ Difficulty timing movement with metronome

MODIFICATIONS

☐ Crawl on elbows.

☐ Work on core and shoulder strength by alternating between elbows and hands, without the crawl, 5-10 times.

- [ ] Give physical cues by either placing the correct arm and leg on the floor or tapping (touching) the side that needs to move.

- [ ] Use verbal cues: tell the child what to do.

- [ ] Visual cues: use visual cues to help a child motor plan (e.g., use stickers on hands and place the same color sticker on the opposite leg that needs to move in unison. Ask the child to move only the same color stickers.

24) SCISSOR JUMPS

MATERIALS: None

1. Start in a standing position.

2. Jump and land with your right arm raised forward and left leg forward, and opposite arm and leg reaching backward.

3. Jump and simultaneously switch legs and arms.

4. Repeat up to 10 times.

GOALS

1. Bilateral coordination

2. Balance

3. Motor planning and timing

4. Posture and strength

5. Visual perception, scanning, and peripheral vision

6. Right- and left-side discrimination

7. Crossing the midline

8. Auditory processing

VARIATION

1. Use metronomes to incorporate auditory processing.

POSITIVE SIGNS

☐ Smooth and coordinated movement pattern

☐ Able to time movement with metronome

☐ Good cross-lateral and oppositional movement (body is able to slightly twist to the opposite side)

NEGATIVE SIGNS

- ☐ Unable to coordinate

- ☐ Jumps but only moves the arms or the legs

- ☐ Jumps but nothing moves

- ☐ Jumps and the entire body turns toward one side

- ☐ Difficulty timing movement with metronome

- ☐ Unable to coordinate cross-lateral and oppositional movement (e.g., lacks the twisting of the body)

MODIFICATIONS

- ☐ Practice placement of legs without the arms (e.g., jump and place right leg forward and left leg back. Then jump and switch.)

- ☐ Practice arms without the legs. You can do this either seated or standing.

- ☐ Visual cues: place the same colored stickers/marks on the opposite arm and leg. Ask the child to move only the same colored arm and leg.

- ☐ Physical cues: give physical cues by touching the correct arm and leg which needs to move.

- ☐ Use only verbal cues.

BALL GAMES:

BOUNCING, CATCHING, HITTING, AND THROWING

The following exercises demand that more than one reflex be integrated. Your child may have some reflexes still retained; therefore, it's necessary to evaluate or screen the child before working with specific exercises. As you continue to introduce new activities, games, or exercises, make sure the child is ready to participate. Remember not to frustrate the child. Make it fun and doable. At the bottom of the exercises, I have provided some modifications, and you can break down each exercise to help the child participate. Some of the modifications include visual, tactile, or physical cues.

In addition to these therapeutic and structured exercises to promote integration, you can also incorporate games and sports that work on the same skills.

25) BALLOON TOSS

MATERIALS: Balloon

1. Give the child an inflated balloon, and toss or bat the balloon overhead for a few minutes.

2. If the child does not have sufficient balance, start in a seated position, and play volleyball.

3. When the child has better balance or is in a cushioned environment, play volleyball with the balloon while standing up.

Balloons are an excellent prop since they travel more slowly than a rubber ball, and give the child more time to react. Encourage the child to look up overhead to hit and catch the balloon.

VARIATIONS

A. <u>Catching</u>: Throw a balloon to the child and play catch. Encourage the use of both hands to catch. This exercise encourages visual tracking (convergence/divergence) and bilateral coordination.

    a. <u>Catching and throwing</u>: After catching the balloon, encourage the child to throw it back to you with both hands. This encourages motor planning and aiming.

    b. <u>Hitting a moving balloon</u>: Instead of catching with both hands, have your child hit the balloon with their dominant hand. You should then pass the balloon back to them. This will help slow down the speed. You can skip this stage, and move to the next, if you think your child is ready and will still have fun.

    c. <u>Hitting the balloon back and forth</u>: Don't stop the balloon, and have the child play volleyball with you.

    d. <u>Throw and catch</u>: Have your child toss the balloon upward and catch it, repeating this several times. This exercise encourages vertical tracking, eye-hand coordination, and motor planning.

    e. <u>Juggle the balloon</u>: Have the child hit the balloon up in the air repeatedly without catching it. This activity can be difficult since it challenges the vestibular system, and kids with balance challenges might have difficulty maintaining their balance. It encourages vertical tracking, speed, motor planning, and body awareness.

f. <u>Alternate hands while hitting a moving balloon</u>: Specify the hand with which you'd like the child to catch the ball. This encourages eye-hand coordination, motor planning, and body awareness.

g. Have fun!

GOALS

1. Bilateral coordination

2. Balance and posture

3. Motor planning and timing

4. Posture and strength

5. Visual perception, scanning, tracking, and peripheral vision

6. Spatial orientation

7. Right- and left-side discrimination

8. Crossing the midline

9. Auditory processing and timing

10. Hand-eye coordination

POSITIVE SIGNS

- [ ] Able to coordinate both sides of the body to catch and hit the balloon

- [ ] Able to sustain smooth and controlled visual tracking skills

NEGATIVE SIGNS

- [ ] Unable to maintain smooth and controlled movement

- [ ] Unable to visually track the balloon

- [ ] Appearing disoriented

- [ ] Dizziness

- [ ] Facial grimaces and movement overflows

26) BOUNCING, THROWING, AND CATCHING BALL

MATERIALS: Tennis ball, racket ball, or any small bouncing ball

1. Start in the standing position.

2. Ask the child to bounce and catch a ball with two hands.

3. Repeat 10 times.

VARIATIONS

1. Throw straight up: Have the child throw the ball straight up in the air and catch it before it hits the ground.

2. Alternate hands: Bounce the ball with one hand, and catch with the other hand.

3. Hit a target: Have the child bounce the ball at a target on a wall and catch it.

4. Ball pass: Have your child bounce pass to a partner or you, and catch it when tossed back.

5. Balance board: Incorporate a balance board game for more challenge.

GOALS

1. Bilateral coordination

2. Balance

3. Motor planning and timing

4. Fine motor development

5. Gross motor development

6. Eye-hand coordination

7. Visual perception, scanning, near-to-far vision, and peripheral vision

8. Right- and left-side discrimination

9. Crossing the midline

POSITIVE SIGNS

☐ Able to coordinate both sides of the body to catch and hit the balloon

☐ Able to sustain smooth and controlled visual tracking skills

NEGATIVE SIGNS

☐ Unable to maintain smooth and controlled movement

☐ Unable to visually track the ball

☐ Appearing disoriented

☐ Dizziness

☐ Falling or losing balance

☐ Facial grimaces and movement overflows

MODIFICATION

☐ Hit, catch, or toss a hanging ball from left to right.

BALANCING GAMES AND ACTIVITIES

In these exercises, you are targeting the sense of balance, the vestibular, and proprioception systems. While balancing on the ground or a balance board, play a variety of games your child prefers. Our goal is to challenge balance and coordination while the head is turning from side to side.

MATERIALS: Balance board, balloon, beanbags, and balls

27) BALANCE ON ONE LEG

MATERIALS: None

1. When the head is turned to the right, ask the child to stand on the left leg.

2. Hold for up to 7-10 seconds.

3. When the head is turned to the left, ask the child to stand on the right leg.

4. Hold for up to 7-10 seconds.

5. Repeat 5-7 times.

POSITIVE SIGNS

☐ Able to balance self on one foot

☐ Able to keep balance when head is turning from side to side

NEGATIVE SIGNS

- ☐ Unable to balance self on one leg

- ☐ Loss of balance when head turns from side to side

- ☐ Difficulty differentiating the right and left sides of the body

MODIFICATIONS

- ☐ Practice standing on one leg without a head turn.

- ☐ Give physical support as needed.

28) BALL THROW, BOUNCE, AND CATCH

MATERIALS: Small ball and balance board

1. Ask the child to toss the ball from one hand to the other without dropping it.

2. Continue tossing back and forth on an arch for 10 times.

3. Bounce and catch with the opposite hand.

4. Bounce at/on a wall or target and catch.

GOALS

1. Bilateral coordination

2. Balance

3. Motor planning and timing

4. Posture and strength

5. Visual perception, tracking, scanning, and peripheral vision

6. Spatial awareness

7. Body awareness

8. Right- and left-side discrimination

9. Crossing the midline

10. Fine motor development

11. Gross motor development

12. Additional reflexes: Palmar (Grasp), Moro, ATNR, TLR, and STNR

POSITIVE SIGNS

☐ Able to toss a ball back and forth with no difficulties

☐ Able to visually track a moving ball

☐ Able to maintain balance when head is turning from side to side

☐ Able to differentiate the right and left sides of the body

NEGATIVE SIGNS

☐ Difficulty visually tracking the ball

☐ Unable to throw and catch

☐ Loss of balance or disorientation

☐ Hesitation, fear, or anxiety

MODIFICATION

☐ Practice the games on the floor before introducing a balance board.

☐ Start with a bigger ball. The smaller the ball, the harder it gets for the child to catch it.

GAMES AND SPORTS

Games and sports (such as martial arts, tennis, baseball, badminton, and the like) will challenge and promote further integration of the Asymmetrical Tonic Neck Reflex. Consider this when structuring your child's extra-curricular activities. Children with retained reflexes will have difficulty in sports and may refuse to participate. You do not want to force them into a game or sport they hate, but consider whether your child can benefit, and which activity might fit well with your child's and your needs. Make sure your child is having fun and developing healthy social skills in the process. Sports can be challenging for an unintegrated body, but if you can prioritize activities that promote integration, it will lead to a better brain development. Have your child move and play as much as possible.

29) BASEBALL

MATERIALS: Baseball, bat, and gloves

1. Ask the child to stand sideways, with head turned either to the left or to the right.

2. The batting hand should be holding the bat correctly, as shown in the picture.

3. Ask the child to hit the ball while standing sideways.

4. Have fun!

Note: If the child is unable to maintain a proper stance, you can use a visual cue on the ground, so they know where to place their feet.

GOALS

1. Bilateral coordination

2. Balance

3. Motor planning and timing

4. Fine motor coordination

5. Gross motor coordination

6. Eye-hand coordination

7. Visual perception, scanning, near-to-far vision, and peripheral vision

8. Right- and left-side discrimination

9. Crossing the midline

10. Spatial orientation

POSITIVE SIGNS

☐ Able to motor plan movement while maintaining proper stance

☐ Able to hit a moving ball while maintaining proper stance

NEGATIVE SIGNS

☐ Unable to motor plan movement

☐ Unable to maintain a proper stance

☐ Unable to track a moving ball

☐ Confusion of right and left sides of the body

MODIFICATIONS

☐ Use visual cues on the ground to help the child know where to stand.

☐ If the child is unable to hit the moving ball, start with a balloon. Have your child hit a moving balloon with a bat. A balloon moves slower and will give the child additional time to respond.

☐ Practice with a t-ball instead of a moving ball. During this time, focus on stance and motor coordination.

30) TENNIS

While playing tennis, the child will have to anticipate where the ball is coming from and going, which requires good visual perception and spatial orientation.

MATERIALS: Tennis ball and a racket

1. Ask the child to hold a tennis racket with a preferred hand.

2. Instruct the child to hit the moving ball using the tennis racket.

3. Encourage the child to cross the midline to hit the ball in either direction.

4. Have fun!

GOALS

1. Bilateral coordination

2. Balance and posture

3. Motor planning and timing

4. Fine motor development

5. Gross motor development

6. Eye-hand coordination

7. Visual perception, scanning, near to far vision, and peripheral vision

8. Right- and left-side discrimination

9. Crossing the midline

10. Spatial orientation

POSITIVE SIGNS

☐ Able to motor plan movement while maintaining proper stance

☐ Able to hit a moving ball while maintaining proper stance

NEGATIVE SIGNS

☐ Unable to motor plan movement

☐ Slow and delayed reaction

☐ Unable to track a moving ball

☐ Unable to cross the midline to hit the moving ball in the opposite side

MODIFICATIONS

- ☐ If the child is unable to hit the moving ball, start with a balloon. Have your child hit a moving balloon with a racket. A balloon moves slower and will give the child additional time to respond.

- ☐ You can also try **Badminton**. The badminton ball/birdie moves slower and will give the child more time to react.

31) HOPSCOTCH

MATERIALS: Chalk and a sidewalk

1. Draw a hopscotch pattern on the ground.

2. Have the child play a simple hopscotch game.

GOALS

1. Bilateral coordination

2. Balance and posture

3. Motor planning and timing

4. Gross motor development

5. Eye-hand coordination

6. Visual skills (perception, scanning, tracking, and peripheral vision)

7. Right- and left-side discrimination

8. Crossing the midline

9. Spatial orientation

10. Other reflexes: Moro, TLR, Leg cross flexion, STNR, Spinal Galant, and ATNR

POSITIVE SIGNS

☐ Able to balance on one foot

☐ Able to motor plan movement independently

☐ Able to hop on one foot

NEGATIVE SIGNS

☐ Loss of balance

☐ Unable to motor plan movement independently

☐ Unable to alternate feet movement

MODIFICATIONS

☐ Physical support: If balance is an issue, hold the child's hand while playing hopscotch.

☐ Start by jumping with both feet before transitioning to one foot.

32) CLIMBING LADDERS AND PLAY STRUCTURES

MATERIALS: Ladder or uneven surfaces

1. Have the child climb a ladder or play structures.

2. Ask the child to alternate hands and feet when climbing.

GOALS

1. Bilateral coordination

2. Balance

3. Motor planning and timing

4. Posture and strength

5. Visual skills (perception, scanning, and peripheral)

6. Right- and left-side discrimination

7. Crossing the midline

8. Fine motor development

9. Gross motor development

10. Additional reflexes: Palmar (Grasp), Moro, TLR, STNR, Spinal Galant, and Leg Cross Flexion-Extension

POSITIVE SIGNS

☐ Able to grasp the ladder and alternate feet to climb

☐ Able to balance self, and climb up and down independently

☐ Able to anticipate where feet should be on the ladder without continually looking down

NEGATIVE SIGNS

☐ Unable to alternate feet to coordinate movement

☐ Confusion and loss of balance or fear

☐ One side preference; the child may only be using one side of the body to climb without alternating feet

MODIFICATION

• Use smaller ladder and play structure

• Give physical support

33) ROCK CLIMBING

Follow the appropriate safety measures for rock climbing. Rock climbing is an advanced sport and requires the integration of a variety of reflexes, including but not limited to the: Palmar (Grasp) Reflex, Moro Reflex, Tonic Labyrinthine Reflex (TLR), Spinal Galant Reflex, and Symmetrical Tonic Neck Reflex (STNR).

MATERIALS: Rock climbing structures, harness, and proper facility

GOALS

1. Bilateral coordination

2. Balance

3. Motor planning and timing

4. Posture and strength

5. Visual skills (scanning, near and far, and peripheral)

6. Body awareness

7. Right- and left-side discrimination

8. Crossing the midline

9. Spacial awareness

10. Fine motor development

11. Gross motor development

12. Additional reflexes: Palmar (Grasp), Moro, TLR, STNR, Spinal Galant, and Leg Cross Flexion-Extension

POSITIVE SIGNS

☐ Able to alternate hands and feet to climb up and down

☐ Able to climb to either side

☐ Adequate hand strength to pull self up

NEGATIVE SIGNS

☐ Unable to alternate hands and legs to properly climb up and down

☐ May be able to climb up but difficult to climb to the side

☐ Confusion and unable to motor plan next movement (e.g., gets stuck and does not know what to do)

MODIFICATIONS

☐ If there is an excessive amount of fear and anxiety, which is disproportionate to the activity, you should first work on the Moro Reflex before introducing this sport.

☐ Practice climbing a ladder.

☐ Practice climbing a play structure.

☐ Physical cues: Tap or touch the foot that needs to move and direct the child where to move it.

34) TUG OF WAR

MATERIALS: Rope

1. Lay out a rope between two teams facing each other in a line.

2. Instruct a member of the opposing teams to tightly grab the end of the rope.

3. Place a mark on the rope and/or on the ground (whichever works for you).

4. Whichever team pulls the rope all the way to the mark or pulls the opposing team past the line on the ground wins.

GOALS

1. Bilateral coordination

2. Balance

3. Motor planning and timing

4. Posture and strength

5. Visual skills (scanning, near and far, and peripheral)

6. Body awareness

7. Right- and left-side discrimination

8. Crossing the midline

9. Spatial awareness

10. Social skills

11. Teamwork

12. Sportsmanship

13. Fine motor development

14. Gross motor development

15. Additional reflexes: Palmar (Grasp), Hands Pulling, STNR, and Spinal Galant

POSITIVE SIGNS

☐ Able to coordinate the movement pattern for pulling

☐ Able to maintain proper stance and coordinate the pulling motion

☐ Able to pull and alternate hands without letting go of the rope

NEGATIVE SIGNS

☐ Difficulty maintaining grasp on the rope

☐ Lets go of the rope when trying to alternate the pulling motion

☐ Confused and does not know how to pull

MODIFICATIONS

☐ To teach the mechanics of pulling, start with pulling heavy objects.

☐ Play a simple pull and push game.

35) DANCE REVOLUTION

MATERIALS: Directional printouts

Visit https://ritp.info/atnr-book to download supplemental worksheets.

1. Place the floor directional marks, as shown in the picture.

2. Place the directional marks on the wall, as directed in the picture.

3. Start the child on the square in the middle.

4. Ask the child to follow the direction on the wall to jump where the arrow points and back to the starting point.

VARIATION

1. Use music or metronome

2. Use smaller prints on one page to encourage visual tracking and reading

GOALS

1. Visual skills (tracking, scanning, near and far, and peripheral)

2. Bilateral coordination

3. Right- and left-side discrimination

4. Motor planning and timing

5. Focus and attention

6. Pre-reading skills

7. Balance

8. Posture

POSITIVE SIGNS

☐ Able to motor plan sequence independently

☐ Able to visually track from left to right

NEGATIVE SIGNS

- ☐ May visually lose place while tracking steps

- ☐ Loss of balance

- ☐ Confusion and disorientation

CHAPTER 5

ADDITIONAL RECOMMENDATIONS AND RESOURCES

A. HOW DO YOU KNOW IF A TREATMENT PLAN AND EXERCISES ARE WORKING?

Parents often view their children subjectively and have a hard time seeing the gradual changes their children are making with treatment. I created a checklist to help parents more objectively see their child's development. The same list can also be used to determine if the treatment plan is not working. At times, a child may regress, and this should prompt the care provider to change the approach to treatment.

To make this routine easier for non-professionals to implement, I have created an additional list for monitoring progress and a letter of encouragement to parents who are working on the ATNR with their child. The following list is one that I created with my children and the students with whom I've worked. Make sure to add other symptoms and areas that you might observe that I have not included. This list can also include goals you are working on or goals parents have that relate to the ATNR. What is on the list depends on the individual child, and the goal is to observe and note visible improvements. After about 6-8 weeks of constant reflex integration exercises, you should begin seeing changes. If, for any reason, there is no improvement, go back and examine your treatment plan.

B. SUGGESTED MOVEMENT BREAKS AND ACTIVITIES TO HELP PROMOTE ASYMMETRICAL TONIC NECK REFLEX (ATNR) INTEGRATION

To help increase the number of opportunities the child gets to practice, incorporate movement breaks that target the ATNR throughout the day. One way to do this is by creating the child's movement breaks to address the ATNR. While creating the child's movement activities, be careful not to frustrate the child by demanding an exercise that is too hard to do. You want the child to ease into movements and preferably initiate the games. Give the child options. These movement breaks should focus on integrating the ATNR gently and gradually. Please use your clinical judgment and knowledge of the child while you are creating this plan. Below are the suggested activities to get you started.

TABLE #2: SUGGESTED ACTIVITIES TO INCORPORATE THROUGHOUT THE DAY

VESTIBULAR	AUDITORY
• Rolling on the ground on a straight line • Balance boards • Ball toss and catch • Swings • Monkeybars • Moro Reflex exercises and games (Please refer to our Moro Reflex book for more recommendations.)	• Use metronome or other verbal cues to slow down or increase speed and follow auditory instructions. • Music therapy, such as the Integrated Listening Systems (iLS) ○ Consult with an occupational therapist if this method is being used.
VISUAL	**MOTOR COORDINATION**

• Balloon and ball games
• Visual cues to help differentiate right and left discrimination
   ○ Bracelet on hands and legs
   ○ Colored cards on the floor
• Visual tracking while standing
• Visual tracking exercises with straight head
   ○ Horizontal
   ○ Circle
   ○ Diagonal
   ○ Infinity
	• Jumping jacks
	• Scissor jumps
	• Cross crawls
	• Climbing
	• Ball games and sports
	• Lizard exercise
	• Fish exercise
	• Hinge exercise
	• All of the exercises in this book can be adapted and used for motor coordination goals.

Table #2: Suggested Activities to
Incorporate During the Day

C. TREATMENT IDEAS FOR OCCUPATIONAL THERAPISTS WORKING IN A CLINICAL SETTING

There are a variety of games and activities you can incorporate to address the ATNR. The challenge may be grading the activity to meet children at their level while maintaining excitement and fun.

- Almost all exercises, games, and tools in the clinic can directly or indirectly work on the ATNR. Use your clinical judgment to set up your treatment session.

- Collaborate with a vision therapist to address the visual skills, and get proper screening to rule out a vision skill problem.

- If you are trained in the following tools, incorporate them in your sessions. Here are some suggestions:

    o Masgutova Method (MNRI)

    o Rhythmic Movement Training (RMTi)

    o Listening programs, such as Integrated Listening Systems (iLs)

    o Interactive Metronome (IM)

    o Brain Gym and other movement exercises you think are beneficial in your clinical settings

D. LETTER TO PARENT/CAREGIVER

Dear Parents,

When the Asymmetrical Tonic Neck Reflex (ATNR) starts to integrate, you will begin to see improvements and changes in your child's development. However, to make the changes that are needed, you should practice the home exercises your occupational therapist assigns for at least 10 minutes per day. If, after six to eight weeks of therapy, you do not see any changes in your child, please contact your occupational therapist. You know your child best and will notice the main areas of growth or lack thereof. To help guide you through the process, here are some things you can look for and observe during your child's treatment:

- Your child may become a lot more coordinated or start to show improvement in movement activities.

- Your child may begin to show good cross-lateral movements, such as cross crawls, scissor jumps and more.

- Your child's reading skills may start to improve. (Note: If visual skills are an issue, please consult a trained vision therapist.)

- Your child may be a lot more interested in joining a game or participating in sports.

- Your child's hand-eye coordination may start to improve (e.g., able to catch, throw, and hit a ball).

- You might see improvement in your child's running stride (i.e., less robotic and more oppositional).

- Your child's balance and stability may improve.

- You may observe improved handwriting skills.

- Your child may become less clumsy.

- You may start to observe better sitting, standing, walking, and running posture.

- Your child may become less frustrated with movement activities.

- Your child's auditory processing may begin to improve (e.g., you might not need to repeat instruction multiple times).

- Your child's speech and articulation skills may begin to improve.

- Your child may become more focused and less distracted.

TABLE #3: ASYMMETRICAL TONIC NECK REFLEX (ATNR) INTEGRATION EXERCISE LOG

	Asymmetrical Tonic Neck Reflex (ATNR) Integration Exercises	Date Introduced	Date Given to Parents	Date Mastered
1				
2				
3				
4				
5				
6				
7				
8				
9				
10				
11				
12				
13				

14			
15			
16			
17			
18			
19			
20			
21			
22			
23			
24			
25			
26			
27			
28			
29			
30			

31				
32				
33				
34				
35				

GLOSSARY

Asymmetrical Tonic Neck Reflex (ATNR): is a primitive reflex pattern that usually emerges in utero, near 18 weeks, is fully present at birth, and integrates approximately six months after birth. The ATNR is an involuntary movement reaction in response to the head turning to the right or to the left. When the head turns to one side, the ATNR causes the arm and leg the head turns toward to extend (stretch) while the opposite arm and leg flex (bend).

Auditory localization: the ability to perceive and locate from where a sound is coming.

Binaural hearing: the ability to hear with both ears equally.

Binocular vision: also known as **eye teaming,** binocular vision is the ability to use both eyes to focus on an object to see a clear, singular image.

Body awareness: is the understanding of where our body parts are in space and how they are moving.

Convergence: an inward movement of both eyes to focus on a single object; also called "binocular vision."

Cross-lateral movements: any movement pattern that requires the use of both parts of the body to coordinate and move simultaneously to execute a purposeful pattern of movements by crossing the midline. Activities, such as walking, running, and crawling, require us to cross the midline of the body.

Divergence: an outward movement of both eyes to focus on an object further away; also called "binocular" vision.

Eye-hand coordination: also known as **hand-eye coordination,** is the ability to process visual input to guide the hands to achieve a specific task (e.g., reaching and grasping).

Eye teaming: also known as **binocular vision,** is the ability to use both eyes to focus on an object to see a clear singular image.

Extension: straightening of body parts.

Flexion: bending of body parts.

Moro Reflex: is a primitive reflex pattern that typically emerges in utero and integrates approximately four months after birth. Moro Reflex is an involuntary reaction to what the brain perceived as an outside threat. The threatening stimuli can come in via touch, sound or the feeling of being dropped, which creates a sense of falling. When the child senses these sensations, the reflex causes the fanning and clenching of fingers, spreading or extending the extremities, followed by a quick flexion of extremities, and crying or anger.

Motor learning: is a neurological ability to learn new movement skills through practice and repetition.

Motor planning: is the ability to understand, plan, and execute multiple-step movement activities in the correct order.

Movement overflow: also known as "motor overflow," is an involuntary movement (motor) pattern observed during voluntary activity. For example, the tongue sticking out or facial grimace during handwriting or balancing activities.

Palmer (grasp) Reflex: is a primitive reflex pattern that emerges in utero at approximately 11 weeks gestation and integrates approximately 12 months after birth. When the infant's palm is stroked or touched at the base of the fingers, the fingers close into a firm grasp starting from the pinky finger.

Peripheral vision: is the eyes' ability to use side vision while gazing straight ahead.

Postural Reflex: are mature patterns of responses that control balance, motor coordination, and sensory-motor development.

Primitive reflexes: are involuntary movement patterns that are present at birth and become dormant or "integrated" before the child reaches

12 months of age. Most reflexes become integrated into a pattern of movement after infancy, so more mature and voluntary movements can emerge.

Proprioceptive input: is an internal sense of **body awareness** that comes from our joints, muscles, tendons, and connective tissues when we move or bear weight on our limbs.

Retained Reflex: is a term used to refer to primitive reflexes that are active in the body when they should have been inhibited (dormant).

Right/Left discrimination: is an internal or external spatial perception, interpretation, and differentiation of sensory information that originated from the left and right sides of the body.

Rooting Reflex: is a primitive reflex pattern that typically emerges in utero and integrates approximately three to four months after birth. When the baby's mouth or cheek is stroked or touched, the head turns toward the stroke, and the mouth opens in search of stimuli. If the mouth finds something to grab, the mouth closes over it, and the sucking motion begins.

Saccade eye movement: is the eye's ability to accurately jump back and forth between targets.

Sensory integration: is a term, developed by Jean Ayers, which explains how the brain receives, perceives, and reacts to sensory information either from inside or outside the body. She defines sensory integration as *"the neurological process that organizes sensation from one's own body and from the environment and makes it possible to use the body effectively within the environment."*

Smooth pursuit: is the eye's ability to smoothly and accurately track a moving object or follow a line.

Spatial orientation: is the brain's ability to orient the body to the ground with or without vision.

Spinal Galant Reflex: is a primitive reflex pattern present in the womb and also present at birth that integrates at approximately 9-12 months of age. When the right or left side of the back below the waist is stroked or touched, this reflex causes the child to side-bend toward the same direction.

Symmetrical Tonic Neck Reflex (STNR): is a primitive reflex pattern that usually emerges in utero and continues to develop after birth. It becomes active at approximately six months of age and starts to integrate at approximately ten months. The STNR is an involuntary reaction to a downward and upward movement of the head. There are two STNR positions. Position 1 is a downward head movement, which causes the elbows to flex and the legs to extend. Position 2 is an upward head movement (also called Sphinx Position), which causes the elbows to extend and the legs to flex.

Tonic Labyrinthine Reflex (TLR): is a primitive reflex pattern that usually emerges in utero and continues to develop after birth. The TLR is an involuntary reaction to the forward and backward movement of the head. There are two types: **TLR Forward** occurs when the head is in front of the spine, causing the arms and legs to flex and tuck inward. **TLR Backward** occurs when the head is behind the line of the spine, causing the arms and the legs to extend, and the back to arch and stiffen.

Vestibular sense: is the body's sense of balance and movement.

Visual tracking: is the ability to maintain a visual gaze on a moving object or a predictable line while reading.

Visual discrimination: is the ability to recognize details in what is being seen while identifying similarities and differences.

RESOURCES

Active Baby, Healthy Brain: 135 Fun Exercises to Maximize Your Child's Brain Development from Birth through age 5½, by Margaret Sasse.

Assessing Neuromotor Readiness for Learning: The INPP Developmental Screening Test and School Intervention Programme, by Sally Goddard.

Brain Gym: Simple ACtivities for Whole Brain Learning, by Paul E. Dennison.

Integration of Infant Dynamic and Postural Reflex Patterns-MNRI (Masgutova Neurosensorimotor Reflex Integration). Svetlana Rihanna Masgutova Ketubah, PhD.

Masgutova Neurosensorimotor Reflex Integration programs https://masgutovamethod.com/

Medical Dictionary: Movement That Heals, by Harald Blomberg, MD.

Neuromotor Immaturity in Children and Adults: The INPP Screening Test for Clinicians and Health Practitioners, by Sally Goddard.

Parents' Guide to Masgutova Neurosensorimotor Reflex Integration (MNRI), by Svetlana Masgutova, PhD. & Denis Masgutova.

Reflexes, Learning and Behavior, by Sally Goddard.

The Misunderstood Child: Understanding and Coping with Your Child's Learning Disabilities, by Larry B. Silver, M.D.

The Out-of-Sync Child: Recognizing and Coping with Sensory Integration Dysfunction, by Carol Stock Kranowitz, M.A.

The Rhythmic Movement Method: A Revolutionary Approach to Improved Health and Well-Being, by Harald Blomberg, MD.

The Symphony of Reflexes: Interventions for Human Development, Autism, CP, and Other Neurological Disorders, by Bonnie L. Brandes Med.

https://medical-dictionary.thefreedictionary.com/

ABOUT THE AUTHOR

Kokeb Girma McDonald is a pediatric occupational therapist and the founder of Polaris Therapy. She is the mother of two wonderful children, and has extensive professional experience working with young people of all ages and backgrounds, since 2004. Recognizing the need for practical and universally accessible primitive-reflex-integration programs, Kokeb created this series to empower and reassure frustrated parents, and to offer fellow professionals a tool to expand their clinical reach. Kokeb's formal education includes a Bachelor's of Science in Occupational Therapy, and a Master's of Science in Health Care Administration, Management, and Change in Health Care Options. She also has additional training in the Masgutova Neurosensorimotor Reflex Integration (MNRI), Integrated Listening Systems (iLs), Interactive Metronome (IM), and Learning Without Tears.

Make a Difference
by leaving a review!

Instructions: Scan the code above, scroll to the bottom of the Amazon product page, and click the "Write a Review" button

Your review helps Reflex Integration Through Play™ reach more parents, therapists, and teachers in need!

I appreciate all of your feedback and love hearing what you have to say. These books are for you! We need your help to make our series better. Thank you for all your support!

OTR/L & Author

Made in United States
Orlando, FL
13 August 2024

50334446R00108